Staying at a Lighthouse

Help Us Keep This Guide Up to Date

Every effort has been made by the author and editors to make this guide as accurate and useful as possible. However, many things can change after a guide is published—establishments close, phone numbers change, facilities come under new management, etc.

We would love to hear from you concerning your experiences with this guide and how you feel it could be improved and kept up to date. While we may not be able to respond to all comments and suggestions, we'll take them to heart and we'll also make certain to share them with the author. Please send your comments and suggestions to the following address:

The Globe Pequot Press
Reader Response/Editorial Department
P.O. Box 480
Guilford, CT 06437

Or you may e-mail us at:
editorial@globe-pequot.com

Thanks for your input, and happy travels!

Staying
at a Lighthouse

America's Romantic and Historic
Lighthouse Inns

BY JOHN GRANT

GUILFORD, CONNECTICUT

Text design: Casey Shain
Photo credits: See page 91, which is a continuation of the copyright page.
Map credits: Rusty Nelson ©The Globe Pequot Press; lighthouse icon courtesy of Rusty Nelson

ISBN 0-7627-2191-X
ISSN 1541-8987

Manufactured in the United States of America
First Edition/Second Printing

The prices and rates listed in this guidebook were confirmed at press time. We recommend, however, that you call establishments to obtain current information before traveling.

CONTENTS

Introduction

Lighthouses have outlived their practical maritime value. While we cling to the hope that these historic beacons continue to help seafarers, the reality of modern technology is that lighthouses are about as useful to a mariner as a manual typewriter is to a writer. Yet we are not ready to give up these now unneeded structures that represent such a fascinating part of our maritime and economic heritage.

In the past few decades, the United States has seen a resurgence of interest in lighthouses. Thousands of individuals and hundreds of groups have rallied to save and restore these stoic structures. We've been fortunate to be able to document many of the heroic efforts made by people around the country to save lighthouses. We've told their stories in ten hours of PBS documentary programs and two *Legendary Lighthouses* books.

As people have rallied to save America's lighthouses, they have also found new uses for them, helping to ensure that they can survive into the future. One of the most intriguing developments is the growing number of lighthouses that provide overnight accommodations. In our research and travels, we've found more than two dozen U.S. lighthouses that offer some sort of overnight experience. These range from elegant bed-and-breakfast inns to hostels to rustic, even spartan, accommodations. Some provide the opportunity for guests to help maintain the lighthouse and experience something of what it might have been like to be a lighthouse keeper.

The one thing the lighthouses described here all have in common is a chance to spend the night, or longer, in a unique setting at a beautiful spot along the American coastline. Charlotte Johnson, executive director of the Rose Island Lighthouse in Rhode Island, sums it up best when she says, "We invite people to go back in time as far as their imaginations can take them."

The types of overnight lighthouse experiences vary widely, but they all add new meaning to the idea of getting away from it all. Lighthouses aren't usually located at the crossroads of America. They tend to be found at the end of a narrow road or path, at the very tip of a peninsula or island, or on a beach that's miles from the nearest paved road. In truth, lighthouses have some of the best beachfront property in America.

Don't expect room service, TVs, or laptop connections at these cozy waterside getaways. In some cases don't even count on indoor plumbing! But you can expect all the quiet you'll need to discover peace and romance. Guests at these lighthouses stay in dwellings that were used by keepers and their families many years ago under much different circumstances.

If you are interested in staying at a lighthouse, spend some time researching the many options. The handful of them that are actual B&Bs offer the most comfortable accommodations, but don't overlook the several places where Hostelling International provides low-cost lodging. And if you're looking for a lighthouse adventure, investigate some of the more rustic offerings. The reality is that there is an overnight lighthouse experience to fit almost every budget and expectation.

Staying at a lighthouse creates a naturally romantic, philosophical frame of mind. It can bring about a sense of connection with the past and a feeling of remoteness that is hard to find elsewhere. Relax and enjoy the escape from the ordinary.

About This Book

We have attempted to include all of the lighthouses we could identify that accept overnight guests. The number of such lighthouses seems to be increasing all the time, so it is very possible that we have missed a few or that others will start accepting guests after we go to print.

We've done everything possible to carefully check and verify the information presented here. However, as with any guidebook, some of the information is going to be dated almost as soon as it is written. For that reason please be sure to check with each of the lighthouses to confirm the most recent information, especially regarding rates. There may also be additional charges at most locations for state and local taxes.

The old keeper's quarters on Isle au Haut, Maine, provide one of the best lighthouse B&B accommodations available along the East Coast.

Isle au Haut Light
Isle au Haut, Maine

The lighthouse was built in 1907 to guide fishermen in and out of the island harbor. Constructed on a mass of volcanic rock known as Robinson Point, the tower's 16-foot brick upper section rests on a 20-foot-high base of granite blocks rising from the edge of the water. An elevated wooden walkway connects the tower to the two-and-a-half story Victorian-style keeper's house.

During a recent restoration of the lighthouse tower, specialists replaced rotten brick and painted and rebuilt architectural details, bringing the tower back to its original appearance. The tower is owned by the town of Isle au Haut and is maintained by the Coast Guard.

STAYING THERE

The Isle au Haut Light, known historically as Robinson Point Lighthouse, is perched on the Atlantic shore on a remote island in an unspoiled corner of Maine. The picturesque tower at the edge of the water and the secluded, adjacent Keeper's House Inn provide a wonderfully relaxing, romantic, and pampered lighthouse getaway.

Guests reach the tiny island from Stonington on the mailboat that serves the island fishing village. The forty-minute trip takes you past several untouched islands and colorful working lobster pots before arriving at the inn's dock.

Innkeepers Jeffrey and Judi Burke have lived in New York City and California and once worked in the Peace Corps. They operated a bed-and-breakfast in Pemaquid Point before moving to Isle au Haut in 1985, where they restored the deteriorating residence and opened the Keeper's House Inn.

"The type of experience people have here usually takes them by surprise," says Jeffrey during an interview for the *Legendary Lighthouses* TV series. "We don't have telephones and [there's] no entertainment. That's the amenity we have: nothing." If you enjoy relaxing in a chair on the lighthouse front lawn and glancing up from a book occasionally to spot a sailboat or lobsterman, this is the place for you.

There are four bedrooms in the main residence, each comfortably furnished with antiques, coastal memorabilia,

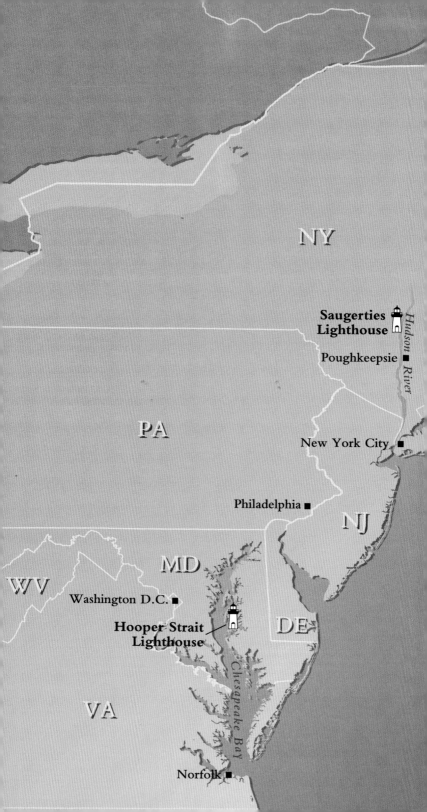

NY

Saugerties Lighthouse

Hudson River

Poughkeepsie ■

PA

New York City ■

Philadelphia ■

NJ

MD

WV

Washington D.C. ■

Hooper Strait Lighthouse

DE

Chesapeake Bay

VA

Norfolk ■

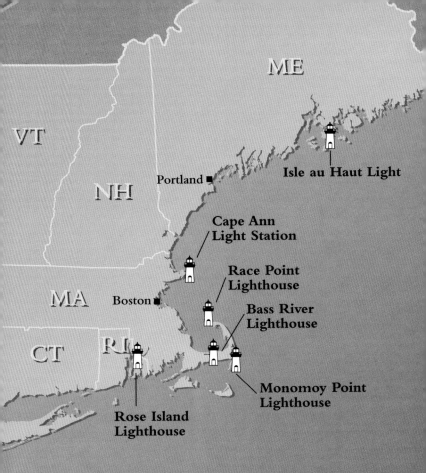

ME

VT

NH

Portland ■

Isle au Haut Light

Cape Ann
Light Station

Race Point
Lighthouse

MA

Boston ■

Bass River
Lighthouse

CT

RI

Monomoy Point
Lighthouse

Rose Island
Lighthouse

ATLANTIC

OCEAN

and island crafts. The only lighting in the bedrooms comes
from candles. Guests share two bathrooms that have hot
water and showers. The Garret Room has water views in two
directions, low ceilings, and a large sitting area. The spacious
Keeper's Room faces the light tower and is equipped with an
old iron bed, sea chest, and potbellied stove. A fifth bedroom
is located in the old Oil House, a tiny dollhouselike cottage
with a private deck on the water.

Great food is a part of the stay at the Keeper's House
Inn. "We try to keep it very simple, kind of homey," says
Judi, who takes the lead preparing three meals a day. "We
pack people's lunches and they walk out the door saying,
'Thanks mom.'"

Candlelight dinners feature fresh native seafood, chick-
en, and a vegetarian selection. No red meat is served. All
breads and desserts are baked daily. Breakfast selections
include homemade honey-sweetened granola and blueberry
pancakes with Maine maple syrup.

The inn relies on a windmill and photovoltaic system to
meet the minimal electrical needs. A large organic garden
provides fresh ingredients for meals. Each morning, Jeffrey
provides an ecotour of the facilities for guests.

The Keeper's House Inn

Isle au Haut Light
P.O. Box 26
Isle au Haut, Maine 04645
(207) 335–2551
www.keepershouse.com

Rooms: Five bedrooms, two bathrooms.

Rates: $294–$335 depending on the room. Rates are per night,
double occupancy. Includes all meals and beverages. A 15
percent service charge covers all gratuities and services.
Boat transportation is $14 per person each way.

Season: Mid-May to mid-October.

Restrictions: No smoking. No pets.

Reservations: Must be made in advance and are accepted by
phone or in writing but not by fax or e-mail. A $100
deposit is required when the reservation is made. Balance
is due thirty days before arrival. Personal checks and
money orders are accepted; no credit cards. Confirmation
of the reservation is sent upon receipt of the deposit.

A 100 percent refund is given with two weeks'

notice of cancellation. Refunds with less than two weeks' notice will be given if accommodations are rerented.

A minimum two-night stay is required from July 1 through September 1 and on all weekends.

Other features: Heat is provided by woodstoves. VHF radio is available for emergency communications. Bicycles and walking sticks are available.

Other information: Arrivals and departures are daily Monday through Saturday. There are no mailboats to the Keeper's House on Sunday or U.S. postal holidays. Guests staying Saturday night also stay Sunday night.

Travel light, because you will need to carry your gear at several stages of the trip to the lighthouse. Boat ramps can be steep at low tide.

Guests may be requested to ration shower time due to occasional water shortages during the summer. Even during summer months evening temperatures can be cool, and trails have wet spots, so bring a jacket, sweater, and good shoes. Dress is very informal. The Keeper's House does not have a liquor license. Guests are welcome to bring their own dinner wine.

To learn more about the inn, the trials and tribulations of getting it started, and life on a Maine island, pick up Jeffrey Burke's award-winning book, *Island Lighthouse Inn: A Chronicle.*

Directions: Take US 1 to Orland. Turn in at the sign to Castine/Deer Isle. Follow State Route 175 south through Penobscot, then State Route 175/15 through Deer Isle and on to the fishing village of Stonington. The 36-mile scenic drive to Stonington from US 1 is an ideal prelude to your trip to Isle au Haut.

THINGS TO DO

The inn is surrounded by mountains, trees, rugged ledges, and incredible island and ocean views. Much of the island is part of **Acadia National Park.** This section of the park is separated by 20 miles of water from the more frequently visited part on Mount Desert Island.

There are many opportunities for hiking through the forest and along the ocean on Isle au Haut. The inn provides bicycles for guests interested in exploring the park or the village, or following the town road around the island to an idyllic swimming pond.

Stonington is the quintessential Maine fishing village.

Allow time to visit the galleries and shops before you leave
on the mailboat or once you return to the mainland.

When the weather is clear, you can see several other
Maine lighthouses in the distance from the perch on the
lighthouse walkway. The Maine coast is dotted with lighthouses on the mainland and nearby islands. It is easy to put
together a travel itinerary that takes you to several of them
in and around your visit to Stonington and Isle au Haut.

Hooper Strait Lighthouse
St. Michaels, Maryland

The traditional tall, shore-based light towers did not work
well around the Chesapeake Bay. A new style of light was
needed to mark the shallow shoals of the bay, and these
lights had to be built over the shoals themselves.

In the 1850s a new technology was developed using iron
piles with blades that could be screwed into the mud. Six or
more of these screws were twisted into the bottom to anchor
a platform for a small keeper's house and light. The cottages
were typically six-sided structures, with the lantern sticking
up through the center of the gabled roof.

Of the more than forty screw-pile light stations that once
marked the Chesapeake Bay, only one—the Thomas Point
Lighthouse just south of Annapolis—remains at its original
location. Many were destroyed over the years by massive ice
floes common on the Chesapeake during the winter.

The original Hooper Strait Lighthouse sank after it was
knocked off its pilings by ice. The current structure was built
in 1879 to mark a key channel. In 1966, when the lighthouse
was replaced by a pole light, the museum stepped in to save
it from demolition. The lighthouse was moved on a barge to
its current location in St. Michaels.

STAYING THERE

Although only one of the original screw-pile lighthouses
built on the Chesapeake Bay is still at its initial location,
several of these structures have been moved onshore in
order to preserve them. One such structure is the Hooper
Strait Lighthouse.

The overnight experience at the Hooper Strait Lighthouse is managed as an educational program by the
Chesapeake Bay Maritime Museum. On selected weekends

during the year, youth groups and families can spend the night at the 1879 lighthouse.

During April, May, September, and October, scout troops, church groups, and other youth organizations can spend Friday and Saturday night in the lighthouse. The groups of ten to fifteen people, including one adult chaperone for every four children, must bring sleeping bags and sleep on the floor. Bathroom facilities are available, and the groups are responsible for their own meals.

The group programs are designed as an educational experience for the children. Participants learn about the lifestyle and duties of lighthouse keepers and take part in some duties, such as learning nautical time, performing maintenance tasks, and recording observations in a log book.

The museum also schedules four or five overnight programs for families at the lighthouse each summer. Called "family overnights," this unique program permits several families to share the lighthouse for the evening. Dinner is provided as part of the fee.

Hooper Strait Lighthouse

The Chesapeake Bay Maritime Museum, Inc.
Mill Street
P.O. Box 636
St. Michaels, Maryland 21663
(410) 745–2916
Fax: (410) 745–6088
www.cbmm.org
E-mail: education@cbmm.org

Rooms: All visitors sleep on the floor in sleeping bags; bathroom facilities are available.

Rates: Per person, $30 for members; $40 for nonmembers.

Season: April, May, September, and October for youth groups, four or five weekends in the summer for family overnights.

Restrictions: Children must be at least eight years old. On family weekends, children must be accompanied by an adult throughout the night.

Reservations: Dates for youth groups are booked one year in advance. Dates for family overnights are set in May each year and registration is on a first-come first-served basis. Interested participants should contact the Education

Department about dates, fees, and registration after May 1.
Reservations are not considered firm until the reservation form and a $50 deposit are received.

Check-in/out: Check-in is at 5:30 P.M.; check-out is by 7:30 A.M.

Other information: To receive an information packet and registration form, call the Education Department, or send an e-mail with your name and address.

Directions: The museum is about a ninety-minute drive east of Washington, D.C. From Washington take US 50 east toward Annapolis, cross the Bay Bridge, and continue to Easton. Just after passing the Easton airport, exit right onto the Easton Bypass/State Route 322 south. At the fourth light turn right onto State Route 33 west. After about 9 miles State Route 33 becomes the main street of St. Michaels. About a half mile into St. Michaels, turn right on Mill Street. The museum parking lot is on the left-hand side of the street.

THINGS TO DO

The **Chesapeake Bay Maritime Museum** has nine exhibit buildings and eighteen waterfront acres in scenic St. Michaels. Visitors can climb aboard the skipjack *Rosie Parks* and imagine the daily drudgery of sailing large wooden boats while hauling up heavy oysters in freezing temperatures and winds.

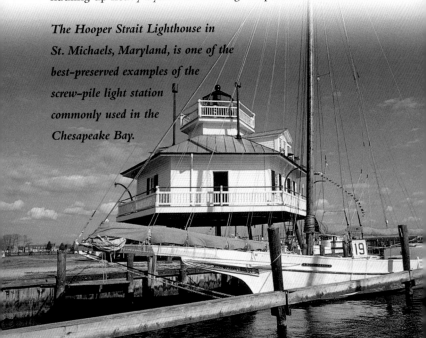

The Hooper Strait Lighthouse in St. Michaels, Maryland, is one of the best-preserved examples of the screw-pile light station commonly used in the Chesapeake Bay.

Also on the grounds is a Potomac River bell that once guided boats through the dense fog. The 1,000-pound bell dates from about 1888. At the center grounds is the 1880 Tolchester Beach bandstand, which once stood at the Tolchester Beach resort, a product of the heyday of steamboats.

For those who love to visit lighthouses, the Chesapeake Bay has much to offer. It is easy to create a driving tour that will take you to several wonderful lighthouses. Many of the Chesapeake's original shore-based lights remain in operation at places like **Cove Point,** Maryland; **Old Point Comfort,** Virginia; and **Jones Point Lighthouse** near Alexandria, Virginia. There are also several other screw-pile lighthouses that have been moved onshore and are accessible to the public. The 1883 Drum Point Lighthouse is on display at the **Calvert Marine Museum** in Solmons, Maryland, and the 1855 Seven Foot Knoll Light can be seen at Baltimore's popular **Inner Harbor.**

 # Bass River Lighthouse
West Dennis, Massachusetts

The Bass River Lighthouse was lit in 1855 to mark the entrance to the commercially important Bass River. After the Cape Cod Canal was opened in 1914, the light was decommissioned and converted to a private residence.

In 1938 the property was purchased by Everett and Gladys Stone and their son Robert, who planned on developing and selling the land. As a way to pay the mortgage that first year, they decided to take in overnight guests. Many of the guests asked to return, prompting the Stones to change their minds about developing the land. The Lighthouse Inn was established, and the Stone family, led by grandson Gregory and his wife Patricia, continues to operate the inn today.

After being dark for seventy-five years, the lighthouse was relit as a privately owned, privately maintained working lighthouse on August 7, 1989. Recognized by the Coast Guard as the West Dennis Light, it operates from May 1 through November 1.

STAYING THERE

The stay at the Lighthouse Inn at the old Bass River Lighthouse on Cape Cod is different than at most lighthouses. The working private lighthouse, now known as the West

Dennis Light, is part of a nine-acre resort complex. Up to 150 guests can stay in a variety of rooms, guest houses, and cottages. Only a few of the rooms are actually part of the original lighthouse.

The old Bass River Lighthouse forms the center section of the present-day Main House at the Lighthouse Inn. The tower rises up from the center of the original 1850s keeper's house. Three small bedrooms, each suitable for one or two people, are all that remain of the original residence. The bedrooms retain the look and feel of the period when they were used by the keeper and his family.

In addition to the three lighthouse bedrooms, there is a wide selection of other accommodations, including cottages with fireplaces, Cape-style houses, and other rooms in the main house. The dining room offers a five-course dinner menu featuring a variety of fresh fish from Cape Cod waters. A full American breakfast is served each morning.

The Lighthouse Inn

Bass River Lighthouse

P.O. Box 128

1 Lighthouse Inn Road

West Dennis, Massachusetts 02670

(508) 398–2244

Fax: (508) 398–5658

www.lighthouseinn.com

E-mail: inquire@lighthouseinn.com

Rooms: There are 68 rooms at the Lighthouse Inn.

Rates: Rates vary for different rooms, houses, and cottages, depending on size, location, and season. Rates range from $218 to $298 per night, double occupancy. Off-season rates are offered between May 17 and June 27 and from September 3 to October 13. Rates include full breakfast and all gratuities. Special packages that include dinner are also available.

Season: Mid-May through mid-October.

Restrictions: No pets.

Reservations: Accepted by phone. A deposit of one night's lodging is required. MasterCard and Visa are accepted. Accommodations are usually booked well in advance. A full refund is given for cancellations made at least fifteen days before the scheduled arrival date.

Check-in/out: Check-in is after 3:00 P.M.; check-out is 11:00 A.M.

Guests arriving earlier or staying later can use the pool house for changing.

Other features: All rooms and cottages have cable TV, telephone, refrigerator, hair dryer, and in-room safe.

The Lighthouse Inn offers modern meeting facilities for up to 120 attendees. Weddings and other social functions can accommodate up to 200 people.

Dress code: Informal during the day; proper dress is requested after 6:00 P.M.

Directions: Cross the Cape Cod Canal on the Bourne or Sagamore Bridge, then take US 6 east to exit 8 (Dennis). Take a right off the exit onto Station Avenue. At the third light turn left onto State Route 28. After about a mile take a right onto School Street, go a half mile, and turn right onto Lighthouse Road. Follow the road 0.2 mile, then turn left onto Lighthouse Inn Road.

THINGS TO DO

The Lighthouse Inn is situated along the shore of **Nantucket Sound.** Guests may enjoy tennis, volleyball, shuffleboard, a game room, an outdoor heated swimming pool, and a 700-foot private beach, plus two adjacent beaches with more than a mile to stroll. During the summer, children's programs are offered.

The inn is convenient to many Cape Cod attractions. Five public eighteen-hole golf courses are located within 5 miles of the inn.

Cape Ann Light Station
Thacher Island, Massachusetts

The lighthouse built on Thacher Island in 1771 was the last of the colonial lighthouses built during British rule. A keeper sympathetic to the British kept the lights dark during the Revolutionary War. They were relit after the war by the state government.

To make the signal different from other Massachusetts lights, two 45-foot stone towers were built. These were also the first American lighthouses to warn ships away from a dangerous spot along the coast; earlier lighthouses were built to guide ships safely into the entrances of ports.

A stone house, which was built on the island in 1816 at a cost of $1,415, still stands today. A fog bell was added at the lighthouse in 1853. Two new towers, both 124 feet tall, were built in 1861. Both lights were fitted with giant first-order Fresnel lenses. A new two-story wood frame keeper's dwelling was built near the north tower, and a two-and-a-half-story brick dwelling was built near the south tower.

The north light was deactivated in 1932. It was relit as a private aid in 1989 and is managed by the Town of Rockport. The south light and fog signal were automated in 1980 and the Fresnel lens removed. The new solar-powered light is managed by the Coast Guard. The Town of Rockport's Thacher Island Committee, in partnership with the Thacher Island Association, maintains and operates the lighthouse accommodations.

STAYING THERE

The first visitors to Thacher Island arrived in the early 1600s. Today the fifty-acre island, located a quarter mile off the Massachusetts coast, greets visitors interested in the austere overnight accommodations at the Cape Ann Light Station, one of America's earliest lighthouse sites.

An apartment in the lighthouse keeper's dwelling can be rented for weekends. The accommodations are very rustic, sort of like camping with a roof over your head. The two-and-a-half-story apartment has three bedrooms, a kitchen with appliances, living room, and bath and shower. The arrangement sleeps two to six people and is rented to only one family, couple, or group per night. There is water for washing and showering, but water supply on the island is limited. Guests must provide their own food and drinking water.

Transportation to the island is provided by the Thacher Island Town Committee launch from the Rockport Harbor. It's a three-mile, fifteen-minute trip and is always contingent upon the weather. Small boats and kayaks can land on the island, and there is a public mooring for use by larger boats on a short-term basis. Anytime there are guests on the island, a keeper is in residence at the lighthouse.

Cape Ann Light Station

Thacher Island Association
18R High Street
Rockport, Massachusetts 01966
(978) 546–7697
www.lighthouse.cc/thacher, www.thacherisland.org

Rooms: Three bedrooms accommodate up to six people in the same party.

Rates: $300 for up to six people for the weekend.

Season: July through mid-September.

Restrictions: No children under five. No pets. Open fires and smoking are prohibited.

Reservations: Advance reservations and a two-night minimum are required. No deposit is required. Pay by check or cash on the date of arrival. No credit cards are accepted.

Check-in/out: Guests are taken out by boat on Friday evening and return to the mainland Sunday afternoon. Exact times are arranged close to the arrival date.

Other features: Sheets, towels, and blankets are provided. There is access to a washer, dryer, and phone in the on-site keeper's residence.

Other information: There is also a small campground available from June 1 to September 1 at a cost of $5.00 per person per night. Campers must make advance reservations by calling the reservation number. Campers often kayak to the island.

Directions: Guests depart from the Rockport Harbor, about an hour north of Boston. From Boston, take US 1 north to Route 128 north to Gloucester. Continue north on State Route 127 to Rockport. Turn right onto Broadway to reach the harbor.

THINGS TO DO

Activities on the island are limited. There is no beach for swimming on the rocky shoreline. There are scenic trails that take visitors past rugged granite ledges, old graveyards, and high gravel bluffs overlooking cobble beaches.

The northern part of the island is owned by the U.S. Fish and Wildlife Service. In the spring the island is home to a nesting colony of herring gulls and great black-backed gulls.

The north lighthouse tower is open to visitors and provides scenic vistas of the Boston skyline 35 miles to the southwest, the shores of New Hampshire, and the peak of Mount Agamenticus on the coast of Maine to the northwest.

Monomoy Point Lighthouse
Chatham, Massachusetts

The lighthouse was built to guide mariners around Monomoy Point, 9 miles south of Chatham. The original light was built in 1823; the current tower and keeper's residence were built in 1849. The light was fitted with a fourth-order Fresnel lens in 1857, and the tower was painted its current red color in 1882.

With the completion of the Cape Cod Canal in 1914 and the increase of power at the Chatham Lighthouse in 1923, Monomoy Point Light was decommissioned. The property was sold into private ownership. The islands, which served as a U.S. Navy bombing range during World War II, are now administered by the U.S. Fish and Wildlife Service.

STAYING THERE

Getting to the Monomoy Point Lighthouse is one of the best and most challenging adventures of any lighthouse accommodations in the United States. Once you get there, the experience is unmatched.

Monomoy is an example of the shifting landscape of Cape Cod. It was once a peninsula extending south from Chatham. In 1880 it became an island, then a few years later a peninsula again. A storm in 1978 cut the 7-mile Monomoy peninsula into two islands. The two islands and a portion of the mainland at what is called the "elbow" of Cape Cod make up the Monomoy National Wildlife Refuge. The refuge's 2,700 acres are protected and managed by the U.S. Fish and Wildlife Service. Ninety-four percent of Monomoy's acreage is designated as a wilderness area.

The Cape Cod Museum of Natural History in Brewster manages the overnight trips to the lighthouse. There is one trip per week starting early Saturday morning and returning Sunday afternoon.

To get to the lighthouse, visitors take a forty-five-minute boat trip from Chatham. Because there is no dock on the island, visitors jump off the boat into knee-deep water, retrieve their gear from the boat, and walk to shore. Then the lighthouse adventure really begins. The lighthouse is located about a mile or so inland. There are no roads, sidewalks, or vehicles. For that matter there are no other buildings on the island. When the light tower comes into view, it truly serves as a beacon for visitors. Overnight guests must carry their own gear and supplies, including drinking water. Pack lightly, and don't bring a suitcase.

The trips are led by a naturalist from the Cape Cod Museum of Natural History, who also provides all meals. The walk to the lighthouse usually takes about an hour. The terrain is fairly flat and the pace is slow. The guide stops several times along the way to point out various types of birds or plant life.

Once at the lighthouse guests inspect their basic overnight accommodations, have lunch, and head out with the naturalist to explore the island. The sea life around the island varies depending on the season. Gray seals and harbor seals can be seen during the spring and fall. In mid-July the fall migration of shorebirds begins, as many birds use Monomoy as a stopover on their way south.

But it is at night that guests staying at the Monomoy Point Lighthouse capture the uniqueness of this experience. Stars in the sky are uninterrupted by anything man-made, and the sounds of nature, including the call of the great horned owl, create a solitude that is unmatched in everyday life. A night spent at the Monomoy Point Lighthouse provides a true sense of the isolation and simplicity of the life of a keeper.

The simple accommodations in the two-story wooden Cape Cod–style keeper's quarters are in keeping with the setting. Guests stay in one of three upstairs bedrooms and must bring their own sleeping bags. Cots and air mattress are provided at the lighthouse. There is no electricity, but there are flush toilets. The kitchen has a table and chairs, but most guests enjoy eating their meals on the outside deck.

Guests have access to the 40-foot brick-lined iron tower. The lens room provides a great vantage point to oversee the island, observe wildlife or passing boats, and watch the sunset.

Monomoy Point Lighthouse

Cape Cod Museum of Natural History
P.O. Box 1710
869 Route 6A
Brewster, Massachusetts 02631
(508) 896–3867
Fax: (508) 896–8844
www.ccmnh.org
E-mail: info@ccmnh.org

Rooms: Three bedrooms, shared bathroom.

Rates: Per person, $180 for museum members; $200 for non-members.

Season: End of June through September 28.

Restrictions: Children must be thirteen or older.

Reservations: Accepted by phone. Preregistration and a $50 deposit are required. MasterCard, Visa, and Discover cards are accepted. The deposit if forfeited with any cancellation. Cancellations within forty-eight hours of scheduled departure forfeit the entire cost.

Check-in/out: Guests depart the museum at 6:30 A.M. on Saturday and get back to the museum around 2:30 P.M. on Sunday.

Other information: It is important to wear long, light-colored pants, even during hot weather, to protect against poison ivy and ticks. Sunscreen is essential, as is insect repellent during greenhead fly season from early July through mid-August.

A backpack is best for your gear, so your hands are free. Binoculars, a flashlight, and a camera are recommended.

Weather is always a factor in getting to the island. Trips may be canceled in case of inclement weather. If the weather is good Saturday but the forecast is bad for Sunday, a one-day trip on Saturday may be substituted for the overnight trip at a lower fee. If that is not possible, a full refund is made.

Directions: Guests depart for the lighthouse from the Cape Cod Museum of Natural History, located at 869 Route 6A in the town of Brewster, about midway on Cape Cod. It is about a forty-minute drive from the Bourne and Sagamore Bridges.

THINGS TO DO

A number of other lighthouses are within easy driving distance of Chatham. The **Chatham Light** sits on a high bluff overlooking the entrance to Chatham Harbor. It now serves as a Coast Guard Station. The **Cape Cod Light,** also known as Highland Light, is Cape Cod's oldest light. The present tower and keeper's house had to be moved back from the edge of a sandy cliff to prevent them from falling into the ocean.

Race Point Lighthouse
Race Point, Massachusetts

The first Race Point Light was built in 1816 after a large number of shipwrecks in the area. The lighthouse was located 2½ miles from Provincetown, but travel was made difficult by the soft sand and many dunes along the route. Race Point was the first of three lighthouses built to guide ships in the Provincetown area. The others were the Long Point Light and the Wood End Light.

The first Race Point Lighthouse was a 20-foot-high rubble stone tower. A fog bell was installed in 1852 and a fourth-order Fresnel lens in 1855. The fog signal was replaced in 1873. The current 40-foot brick-lined cast iron tower and the oil house were built in 1876. When electricity was installed in 1957, the Fresnel lens was replaced with an electric bulb. In 1960–61 the larger of the two keeper's houses was torn down. The light was automated in 1978 with a solar-powered optic.

For almost twenty years after the Coast Guard left, the keeper's house was boarded up. "This is the one that was forgotten," says Jim Walker, who heads a dedicated group of volunteers who restored the lighthouse structures. The work was done a little at a time over many years, but the results seem worth the effort. "To spend a night here and watch the sunset," says Walker, "is worth an awful lot of work."

STAYING THERE

Reaching 70 miles into the Atlantic Ocean, Cape Cod is a formidable obstacle to navigation. Over the course of the nineteenth century, eighteen lighthouses were built around Cape Cod, and the handful that remain represent one of the most accessible collections of coastal lighthouses in the country. The Race Point Lighthouse sits at the northwestern tip of Cape Cod along one of the worst stretches for shipwrecks on the Atlantic coast.

Race Point is among the string of beaches that form the Cape Cod National Seashore, one of the most heavily visited summer tourist areas along the Atlantic shoreline. Heavy traffic and crowded beaches can make it difficult to discover the natural beauty and serenity that are the cape's greatest attraction.

Staying at the Race Point Lighthouse is one way to solve the problem of crowded beaches and roads. Race Point is one

The Race Point Lighthouse is located along a remote stretch of the Cape Cod National Seashore.

of the most out-of-the-way spots on Cape Cod. Its isolation once made it an unpopular duty station for lighthouse keepers. Today, guests are driven by four-wheel-drive vehicle across 2 miles of sandy beaches and dunes to get to the lighthouse.

You are surrounded by the ocean and beach when you stay at the Race Point Lighthouse. Located at the point of the hook that forms the very end of Cape Cod, Race Point Lighthouse offers rooms overlooking the Atlantic Ocean and Cape Cod Bay. It is one of the few places on the East Coast where it is possible to see the sun set over the ocean. Race Point also has some of the Cape's best beaches for swimming, fishing, and beachcombing.

Guests stay in one of three upstairs bedrooms in the fully restored keeper's house. The Green Room is the largest, with two double beds and one single bed. The Yellow and Blue Rooms each have one double and one single bed. Guests share a full bathroom upstairs and a half bath downstairs. There is a large common kitchen with two refrigerators, and a cozy living room with sofas and overstuffed chairs. Guests must bring their own food, bed linens, and water.

There is limited electricity at the house. Lighting is provided by gas lanterns. All of the appliances are gas, and well water is used for all washing. Bottled water is used for drinking.

Race Point Lighthouse

New England Lighthouse Foundation

P.O. Box 570

North Truro, Massachusetts 02652

(508) 487–9930

www.racepointlighthouse.net

E-mail: racepointlighthouse@attbi.com

Rooms: Three bedrooms, shared bathrooms. Maximum occupancy is ten people.

Rates: $135–$155 per night, double occupancy; $25 for each additional person.

Season: May 1 to September 30.

Restrictions: No pets. No smoking in the house.

Reservations: Advance reservations are required and are accepted by phone or e-mail. A 10 percent deposit is required to hold reservation. Cancellations prior to seven days in advance of stay received a refund minus a 10 percent fee.

Check-in/out: A meeting time and place is established once you make reservations.

Other features: A host stays in the lighthouse at all times to operate the generator and manage the facility. Guests have access to the light tower.

Other information: The lighthouse is located 2 miles across sandy beaches and dunes. Transportation to and from the lighthouse is provided at the beginning and end of the stay in a four-wheel-drive vehicle. Once at the lighthouse, no transportation is provided.

Directions: Take U.S. Highway 6 almost to Provincetown. Turn north on Race Point Road, continue past the Province Lands Visitor Center, and follow Race Point Road to the end. There is parking near the ranger station. The lighthouse is located 2 miles down the sandy beach.

THINGS TO DO

Whale sightings, seals, shorebirds, and sunsets over the ocean all add to the enjoyment of staying at the Race Point Lighthouse. While we were at Race Point taping for the *Legendary Lighthouses* TV series, the broken wooden hull of a small vessel washed up on shore.

The **Cape Cod National Seashore** is made up of 50 miles of dunes, marsh, sandy beaches, and coastline stretching from Provincetown south to Chatham. The federally protected area consists of constantly shifting beaches and barrier splits, eroding cliffs, sand dunes, and wetlands.

There are more than 44,000 acres within the seashore, including six protected ocean beaches with parking, bathhouse facilities, and visitor centers. There is a wide variety of self-guided and ranger-led walking tours that provide an excellent way to discover the diversity and beauty of the National Seashore. The **Salt Pond Visitors Center** on U.S.Highway 6 in Eastham is a good starting point.

 ## Saugerties Lighthouse
Saugerties, New York

Saugerties was once a major port along the Hudson River, with daily passenger boats traveling to Manhattan. The first lighthouse was built here in 1838 to guide ships away from the nearby shallows and into Esopus Creek. It used five whale oil lamps with parabolic reflectors. The foundation of the original structure can be seen on a small island adjacent to the present lighthouse, which was built in 1869 on a massive stone base 60 feet in diameter. A fourth-order Fresnel lens using kerosene lamps was installed, and in 1910 a fog bell was added to the lighthouse.

The last keeper was removed when the lighthouse was automated in 1954. The abandoned building fell into disrepair, but in 1978 several local citizens succeeded in having the lighthouse added to the National Register of Historic Places. In 1986 the Saugerties Lighthouse Conservancy acquired the lighthouse and adjacent wetlands and began an extensive fund-raising and restoration project. More than 10,000 new bricks were needed to replace those that had crumbled. The entire masonry structure, including the massive stone base, was reconstructed. All of the materials were hauled to the site by barge.

On August 4, 1990, the Coast Guard installed a solar-powered light, returning the lighthouse to operation after thirty-six years. A replica picket fence surrounding the lighthouse contains the names of the keepers who lived and worked at the lighthouse and the hundreds of donors who contributed toward the restoration.

STAYING THERE

At one time sixteen lighthouses marked the commercially important Hudson River. Of the handful that survive today, one invites visitors to spend the night along one of America's most beautiful and historic waterways. The Saugerties Lighthouse sits in isolated splendor along the Hudson River, surrounded by wetlands and water.

Most guests get to the Saugerties Lighthouse along a beautiful half-mile nature trail that starts in a hardwood forest, meanders over bridges and lowlands and through tall stands of cattails and reeds that tower over hikers during the summer, before emerging along the riverbank. Parts of the trail may be under water during high tide, so be sure to check with the keeper for the tide schedule before your arrival.

Guests can also arrive by boat. Larger boats can tie up at the floating dock. A fixed dock is also available, but care is required when tying up to it because of wakes from the river and the rise and fall of the tide. Be sure to let the keeper know in advance if you plan to arrive by boat.

The accommodations at the lighthouse are simple but

comfortable. Both second-floor bedrooms have double beds. The smaller West Room faces both the Hudson River and Esopus Creek. The larger East Room faces the river and can accommodate two air mattresses for children. Guests share a downstairs bathroom with a sink, shower, and hot running water. A composting toilet is used.

The lighthouse is decorated somewhat as it was around 1910. Guests can enjoy supper at one of several local restaurants or carry the fixings for a meal at the lighthouse, where they have access to the parlor, the kitchen, and the refrigerator. There is a gas grill for cooking outside, and there's a stove in the kitchen.

Several delightful spots around the lighthouse provide opportunities to relax, enjoy a book, or just watch the activity on the wide river. The best views are from the tower of the lighthouse, which offers panoramic vistas of the Hudson River with the Catskills looming to the west.

Visitors can explore the lighthouse grounds and island between 2:00 and 5:00 P.M. on weekends and holidays between Memorial Day and Columbus Day. The recommended fee is $3.00 for adults and $1.00 for children. A shuttle boat service operates during those times for those who prefer to travel to the lighthouse by the water route. The lighthouse trail is open year-round.

The Saugerties Lighthouse juts out into New York's Hudson River.

Saugerties Lighthouse Conservancy, Inc.

P.O. Box 654
Saugerties, New York 12477
(845) 247–0656
www.saugertieslighthouse.com

Rooms: Two bedrooms with double beds, shared bathroom.

Rates: $160 for a double room, including breakfast; $35 extra per child. A 10 percent discount is offered for members of the Conservancy.

Season: Year-round.

Restrictions: The electricity supply at the lighthouse is limited; no hair dryers are permitted. No smoking is allowed inside the lighthouse. Pets are permitted only if both rooms are rented by the pet owner or if one room is vacant. A $25 fee is charged for pets.

Reservations: Contact the keeper by phone or check the Web site for availability; reservations are accepted only by phone. A credit card or check is required to hold the reservation. Visa, MasterCard, Discover, and American Express are accepted. A confirmation will be sent by U.S. mail.

All overnight cancellations are subject to a $15 service charge. Cancellations made with less than thirty days' notice are refunded only if the room can be rebooked. If severe weather forces a cancellation, a complete refund is made.

Check-in/out: Normal check-in is after 2:00 P.M. and check-out is by noon, but these times are flexible because of tides.

Other features: Linens, towels, and soap are provided.

Other information: Appropriate footwear for use on the trail varies with the seasons and tides. Waterproof boots are useful much of the time, but sandals can be fine in the summer.

Pack lightly for the trip, bringing a minimum of extra clothing and supplies. For easiest travel carry a backpack so your hands are free during the hike along the nature trail.

Directions: Saugerties Lighthouse is about 100 miles north of New York's George Washington Bridge and about 45 miles south of Albany. The easiest way to reach the lighthouse is from the New York State Thruway, also known as I–87.

Northbound on I–87, get off at exit 20 and turn right at the traffic light. Follow State Route 212 into the center of the village of Saugerties, then proceed straight on US 9W north for four blocks. At the T intersection, turn right onto Mynderse Street. Follow the road and bear left at the stop sign. Proceed down the hill to the lighthouse parking lot, which is just beyond the Coast Guard Station.

Southbound on I-87, get off at exit 20 and turn left onto State Route 32 after paying the toll. A short distance later, turn left onto State Route 212 into the village of Saugerties, then follow the directions above.

THINGS TO DO

The major activity at the lighthouse is relaxing. Swimming off the sandy beaches is possible during warm weather. A small museum in the lighthouse and a videotape provide more details of the history and restoration of the structure.

Saugerties is one of many attractive Hudson River communities. The eight-block commercial section has been designated a National Historic District and is home to more than thirty antique shops. There are plenty of good restaurants within walking distance of the downtown area. Saugerties is also a gateway to the entire Mid-Hudson Valley.

Rose Island Lighthouse
Newport, Rhode Island

The Rose Island Lighthouse was lit in 1870 to warn ships away from the rocky island and to guide them into Newport Harbor and the channel that leads to the busy docks at Providence. A red light on the Newport Bridge made the lighthouse obsolete; it was closed in 1970.

For more than a dozen years, the abandoned lighthouse was a victim of neglect, weather, birds, and vandalism. It became such a eyesore that there was talk of tearing down the structure. Instead, a group of local citizens fought to save and restore the lighthouse to its former stature.

It took the Rose Island Lighthouse Foundation eight years to rally the community, raise money, and refurbish the lighthouse. By 1993 work on the lighthouse and tower was completed, and Rose Island was reestablished as a private aid to navigation.

STAYING THERE

Located a mile offshore on a rocky island in Narragansett Bay, the Rose Island Lighthouse takes guests back in time to learn about life at a lighthouse and participate in preserving a piece of Rhode Island's maritime history. "We let everyone take care of not only themselves but the lighthouse while they're here," says executive director Charlotte Johnson in the *Staying at a Lighthouse* TV program.

The wood framed lighthouse, with its 20-foot tower rising from the top of the roof, has an extensive educational program that includes opportunities for guests to serve as actual keepers for a day or a week. Guests perform a variety of chores during their stay on the island.

The Rose Island Lighthouse is a "living museum" that looks and operates much as it did a century ago. The lighthouse relies on wind power and rainwater, and guests get a glimpse of the uniquely independent way of life of past keepers and their families. The lighthouse museum is used during the spring and fall for school groups and in the summer for public tours.

Guests can spend a single night at the lighthouse in one of two museum bedrooms on the first floor. These original keeper's bedrooms are available for use once the museum closes at 4:00 P.M. The bedrooms are fully furnished, and the kitchen comes complete with pots, pans, dishes, and utensils. Guests must change the beds and put the rooms back in order before the museum reopens at 10:00 A.M. Cleaning supplies and fresh linens are provided.

Each of the museum bedrooms accommodates two people in a double bed. Washbowls and pitchers are provided for bathing, along with bottled water for drinking. Overnight guests must pack a cooler with food and beverages for dinner and breakfast.

Rose Island Lighthouse also offers a "Keeper for a Week" option. Up to four people can stay in the modern second-floor keeper's apartment. Families especially enjoy this lighthouse adventure. Guests who spend a week at the lighthouse must be willing to conserve water and electricity and agree to daily responsibilities and seasonal work projects.

The keeper's apartment is fully furnished with linens, pots, pans, dishes and utensils. The bathroom has a tub/shower and low-flow toilet. There is a queen-size bed and a double sofa bed. Guests must bring their own food.

Weekly guests receive an orientation about the lighthouse, responsibilities, and chores. Each day begins with

The Rose Island Lighthouse is one of many historical structures found in Newport, Rhode Island.

raising the flag and recording weather, electric, and water data. Depending on the season and their skills, keepers' responsibilities include greeting visitors, cleaning, gardening, mowing, painting, and organizing projects to maintain the light station and grounds.

"Probably one of the neatest things," says Charlotte Johnson, "is seeing how satisfied people are with themselves when they leave."

Rose Island Lighthouse Foundation

P.O. Box 1419

Newport, Rhode Island 02840

(401) 847–4242 (weekdays, 9:00 A.M.–1:00 P.M.)

Fax: (401) 847–7262

www.roseislandlighthouse.org, www.roseisland.org

Rooms: Two bedrooms on the first floor; each room accommodates two people. These Museum Rooms are rented for one night only, except from November through March, when you may stay for more than one night.

The Keeper's Apartment on the second floor accommodates up to four people. Weekly stays run Saturday to Saturday.

Rates: Museum Rooms: April–June and September–October, $155 weekdays, $165 weekends; July–Labor Day, $175 weekdays, $185 weekends; November–March, $145 weekdays, $155 weekends.

Apartment: April–June, $1,200 per week; July–August, $1,600 per week; September–October, $1500 per week; November–March, $850 per week.

Rates are based on two adults and their children under eighteen years old; additional adults pay $25 per night. There is no extra charge for children under eighteen who do work and bring their own sleeping bags.

Round-trip boat transportation is provided for $12 per person. Secured parking is available.

Season: Year-round.

Restrictions: No Styrofoam products are allowed on the island. No smoking or candles in the lighthouse. Generally suitable for children ages five and up. No pets April 1–August 15 while birds are nesting; pets allowed at other times with prior approval.

Reservations: The phone is the best way to make reservations and check on availability. The Web site shows availability of both types of lodging. The lighthouse, especially for weeklong stays, is often booked well in advance. Deposit, payment, cancellation, and refund policies differ for each type of lodging. MasterCard, Visa, personal checks, and traveler's checks are accepted. A minimum fee of $50 is retained for canceled or changed reservation dates. Full payment is due if reservations are canceled with less than two months' notice and the rooms cannot be rebooked.

Check-in/out: Varies and is confirmed closer to date of arrival.

Other features: A radiant oil heating system in the floor keeps the lighthouse warm and comfortable, even on the coldest, stormiest winter days. The wind produces enough pollution-free electricity for the fluorescent bulbs. Rainwater for cooking, bathing, and housecleaning comes from the basement cistern. Bottled water is provided for drinking. There are low-flow toilets and solar showers available. In cold weather guests use a shared indoor toilet that is pumped by hand. Propane fuels the cooking stove, hot water, and barbecue grill. A cellular phone and VHF marine radio are provided for emergencies.

Other information: If the weather is too rough to get you safely to the lighthouse, your options are to be put up in town, to reschedule your visit, or to get a gift certificate for the full amount paid. If you are at the lighthouse when the weather turns bad, be prepared to spend an extra night for free.

Directions: Rose Island is located a mile offshore, just south of the Newport Bridge. It is accessible by boat from Newport and Jamestown, depending on the season. The lighthouse office staff will provide directions to the pick-up point.

THINGS TO DO

Rose Island teems with bird life and blooms abundantly with wildflowers. Seals visit in the cooler months, and there is an endless parade of ships and yachts on Narragansett Bay. Guests may fish or swim or explore the beaches.

The sense of traveling to another era is enhanced by a visit to nearby **Newport.** Grand summer mansions, built by the very rich during the Gilded Age, are found throughout Newport. The most magnificent is **The Breakers,** a seventy-room Italian Renaissance home built for Cornelius Vanderbilt II in 1895. The **Trinity Church** has been in continuous use since 1726. The **Hunter House** is considered one of the most beautiful eighteenth-century mansions in America.

Alaska Lighthouses

Petersburg, Auke Bay, and Admiralty Island

Alaska has 33,000 miles of rocky, twisted coastline, yet it has fewer lighthouses, mile for mile, than any place in the United States. Only about a dozen lights mark the Alaska coastline. Most were built in the early 1900s after gold was discovered in Alaska.

Lighthouses in Alaska are very difficult to visit. They are not accessible by car or by walking but must be reached by boat, helicopter, or seaplane. Weather is always an issue when traveling to these very remote locations.

Despite these obstacles, a number of Alaska lighthouses are starting to provide overnight accommodations for visitors. In recent years, many of Alaska's lighthouses have been turned over to organizations for maintenance and preservation. If you are interested in staying at an Alaska lighthouse, it is best to make contact with one of the organizations to determine exactly what type of accommodations are available, when they are available, and at what cost.

The number of Alaska lighthouses offering overnight stays is always changing, as are the logistics of each trip and location. In addition to the lighthouses mentioned here, others are hoping to be able to offer overnight guest accommodations in the future. Those locations include Cape St. Elias Lighthouse, Eldred Rock Lighthouse, and Cape Decision Lighthouse. Often the best way to keep informed about the overnight activities at a lighthouse is to join its organization.

Each of Alaska's lighthouses offers an unbelievable wilderness experience, unparalleled in the lower forty-eight states. Staying at an Alaska lighthouse would be a memorable addition to any visit to the Last Frontier. However, as with just about everything else in Alaska, be prepared for a demanding journey and logistical challenges that require some special arrangements. If you can make it work, it is worth the effort.

Five Finger Island Lighthouse is located on a long, slender scrap of rock rising from the crystal waters of Frederick Sound to the north of Petersburg. Its white

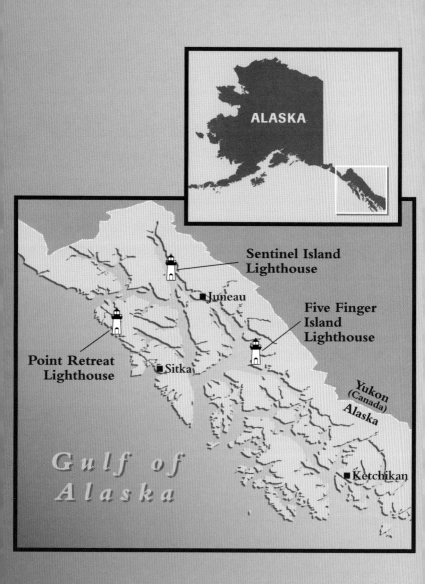

ALASKA

Sentinel Island
Lighthouse

Juneau

Five Finger
Island
Lighthouse

Point Retreat
Lighthouse

Sitka

Yukon
(Canada)
Alaska

Gulf of
Alaska

Ketchikan

PACIFIC
OCEAN

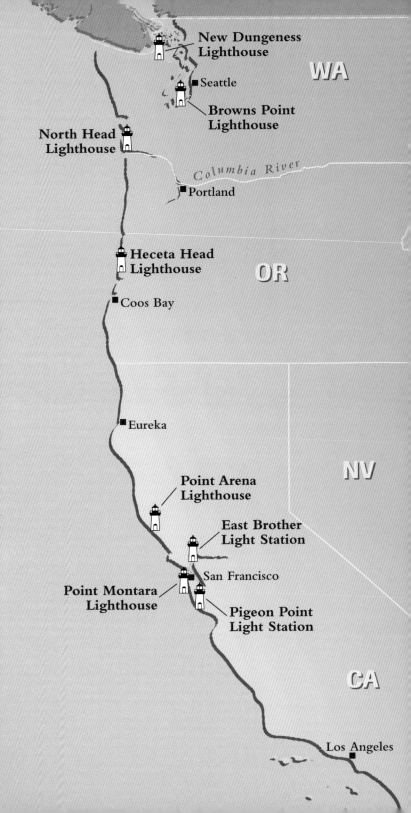

New Dungeness Lighthouse

WA

Seattle

Browns Point Lighthouse

North Head Lighthouse

Columbia River

Portland

Heceta Head Lighthouse

OR

Coos Bay

Eureka

NV

Point Arena Lighthouse

East Brother Light Station

San Francisco

Point Montara Lighthouse

Pigeon Point Light Station

CA

Los Angeles

Like all of Alaska's lighthouses, the structure at Five Finger Island is only accessible by boat, floatplane, or helicopter.

deco-style tower is visible to passengers on ferries, luxury liners, and tour boats as they make their way up and down Alaska's scenic Inside Passage.

The lighthouse, built in 1902, is Alaska's oldest lighthouse and last unmanned site. It was decommissioned in 1984. The original two-story combination tower and residence was a Victorian-style wooden structure with a small lantern room perched on the roof. Burned in 1933, it was replaced by the current reinforced concrete structure. The art deco styling is typical of Alaskan lighthouses.

Five Finger Island is 63 miles south of Juneau at the mouth of Stephen's Passage. The only way to get there is by floatplane, helicopter, or boat.

Sleeping accommodations at the lighthouse are rustic but homey. There are four bedrooms and various nooks and crannies in the keeper's cottage. There is also a living room, kitchen, bathroom, and radio room. The lawn outside is also available for sleeping under the stars. Other buildings include a boathouse, carpenter shed, and hoist house.

The center of the island holds a small rain forest, a microcosm in itself, containing wildflowers, berries, eagle nests, and large hemlock and spruce trees that shelter fragile moss-covered undergrowth. The island perimeter is made of rocky slate cliffs that host numerous seabirds. The view from the cupola on top of the 68-foot tower commands a 360-degree view of the mainland, dozens of neighboring islands, sea mammals that inhabit the area, and mountains that touch the sea. It is common to see whales breach and bald eagles circle the rocky island.

Five Finger Island Lighthouse

Juneau Lighthouse Association
P.O. Box 22161
Juneau, Alaska 99802
(907) 364–3632
5fingerlighthouse.com
E-mail: jenniferklein@gci.net

Sentinel Island Lighthouse is located on six acres of pure Alaskan wilderness. It is the site of one of the first two Alaskan lighthouses that were lit in 1902. The existing 50-foot-tall, art deco–style concrete tower was constructed in 1935, replacing the original tower and keeper's residence.

The lighthouse and island are leased to the Gastineau Channel Historical Society, a nonprofit volunteer organization interested in preserving the lighthouse and making it available to the public. Overnight adventures to Sentinel Island Lighthouse are available for a modest fee.

The accommodations are clean and comfortable but described as remote and cabin style with bunk beds. Guests are asked to bring their own sleeping bags and pads. If long-distance travel makes that difficult, arrangements for sleeping gear can be made. Guests must bring their own food. Cooking gear, water, portable heaters, and emergency equipment are provided. Transportation to the island is by helicopter or boat; the cost depends on the number of passengers and length of stay.

The lighthouse is located in a spectacular setting rivaling any in North America, with forests, towering mountain peaks, and hanging glaciers providing the backdrop. The lighthouse tower's cupola is a special place to visit. "It's about 60 feet above the water, so you get quite a commanding 360-degree view," says Gary Gillette of the historical society. "On

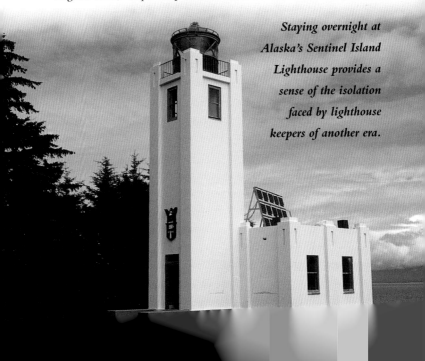

Staying overnight at Alaska's Sentinel Island Lighthouse provides a sense of the isolation faced by lighthouse keepers of another era.

a sunny day you can see glaciers, mountains, and wildlife. But even on a day when we've got winds and rain dripping on the windows, it's still very romantic."

Sentinel Island Lighthouse

Gastineau Channel Historical Society

P.O. Box 21264

Juneau, Alaska 99802

(907) 586–5338

Fax: (907) 586–5820

E-mail: glrrlg@alaska.net

Point Retreat Lighthouse sits at the confluence of two shipping channels in southeast Alaska's vast maze of islands and waterways known as the Inside Passage. It sits at the northern tip of the hundred-mile-long Admiralty Island, a wilderness rain forest that is home to abundant wildlife. Bald eagles frequently perch on the light tower, and brown bears can occasionally be seen in the woods or on the beach. Humpback and orca whales are routinely seen from the dock or light tower. Otters live just south of the dock, and sea lions and harbor seals feed all around the point.

The first lighthouse was established here in 1904 to mark a busy maritime intersection where freighters, ferries, and passenger lines often crossed paths as they traveled between the Inside Passage and the capital city of Juneau. The present buildings date to 1923–24.

When the Alaska Lighthouse Foundation, a nonprofit historical preservation organization, took over the lighthouse, it was in bad shape. "When the Coast Guard decommissioned the light station in 1974, they pulled everything out of here," Dave Benton, president of the association, told us during the taping of *Legendary Lighthouses II*.

Over the years the group of volunteers has reinstalled the utilities and restored the buildings, in spite of the obstacles of distance and transportation. "It's about 17 miles from Juneau to Point Retreat," says Benton, "and we haul everything out here in a skiff and fishing boat."

The association has made enough progress that it now has the lighthouse manned year-round by a volunteer keeper. The group is especially proud of this accomplishment because it has been thirty years since Point Retreat Lighthouse has been manned on a continuous basis.

With such success Point Retreat Lighthouse is hoping to begin accepting overnight guests in the Keeper's Quarters.

Point Retreat Lighthouse sits on an island along the heavily used Inside Passage waterway.

The experience is rustic but with some amenities. The house is furnished with antique furniture and lots of maritime memorabilia, including a claw-foot tub/shower. There is a full kitchen with all meals served.

The best way to learn more about the accommodations is by writing to the association.

Point Retreat Lighthouse
Alaska Lighthouse Foundation
P.O. Box 240149
Douglas, Alaska 99824

 # East Brother Light Station
Point Richmond, California

Even with today's satellite positioning, ships must be on guard against the swift currents and shoals that mark many areas of San Francisco Bay. When the lighthouse at East Brother was built in 1874, it was considered the height of modern technology.

The East Brother Light Station is one of several that marked San Francisco Bay. Most were automated in the 1960s, a modernization that East Brother barely survived. The decision by the Coast Guard to automate the light station was accompanied by a plan to tear down the buildings on the island.

Local residents fought to keep the landmark structures,

and in 1971 the light station was placed on the National Register of Historic Places. Although the structures were saved, they were not protected. Like many other lighthouses around the country, the structures fell into serious disrepair.

In 1979 a local group was formed with the goal of restoring the light station and making it accessible for public use. By that time, neglect, weather, vandalism, and birds had caused significant damage. A $300,000 restoration was completed in 1980. The money represents only a small part of the total cost, as thousands of volunteers pitched in to save the lighthouse.

Volunteers continue to maintain the lighthouse. Day-use fees and the operation of the B&B contribute to the upkeep. The lighthouse Web site contains a lot of information about the history and restoration of the light station, as well as photos and information about staying at the lighthouse.

STAYING THERE

The combination of lighthouse lodging, tiny island, and proximity to San Francisco make East Brother Light Station Bed and Breakfast a distinctive getaway. The single-acre island that is home to the lighthouse B&B is a quarter mile

East Brother Light Station is in San Francisco Bay.

offshore in the straits that divide San Francisco and San Pueblo Bays.

Guests stay in the same building that houses the light. Although lighthouses often have separate structures for tower and keeper's residence, at East Brother the light tower rises up through the center of the Victorian-style keeper's house. According to the innkeepers, a lot of marriage proposals and other life-changing experiences take place during sunsets in the lens room.

The seclusion of the island lighthouse makes it an especially romantic place. There is little to do but savor the food and wine, relish the scenery, enjoy a book, and relax. A great one- or two-day getaway, many people come here for special occasions such as birthdays and anniversaries.

Like the earliest keepers, visitors today arrive by boat.
The trip takes about ten minutes and is described as "an
adventuresome outdoor experience." Accessing the island
requires the physical stamina and strength to climb from a
bobbing boat up a vertical ladder 4 to 12 feet in height
(depending on the tide). Wear sturdy shoes for the climb,
and bring a rain jacket for water spray.

There are four bedrooms in the lighthouse, each with a
queen-size bed and period furnishings. A smaller bedroom in
the Fog Signal Building has a full-size bed and is decorated
in a nautical theme. Some bedrooms have a private bathroom; others share a bath. Guests may relax in the upstairs
and downstairs parlors or on the patio courtyard. There is
plenty of reading material available at the lighthouse, including an illustrated history of the restoration project.

Even though all supplies are brought to the island by
boat, the food is a highlight of the experience. Hors d'oeuvres and champagne are served in the upstairs parlor, and
guests enjoy a four-course dinner in the upstairs dining
room. The menus and wines change with the seasons.

The smell of brewing coffee and freshly baked popovers
(an East Brother specialty) provide a subtle wake-up call.
Coffee is on by 6:30 A.M., the piping hot popovers are ready
by 8:00, and a full breakfast is served at 9:00. Breakfast
includes Lighthouse French Toast Soufflé, another house
specialty. Lunch is provided for guests staying two or more
nights.

Between October 1 and April 1, the lighthouse foghorn
operates twenty-four hours a day, giving a short blast every
thirty seconds. Although most people become accustomed to
the noise and accept it as an interesting aspect of the lighthouse experience, it can be a problem for light sleepers.
Earplugs are the only assistance available.

East Brother Light Station, Inc.

117 Park Place
Point Richmond, California 94801
(510) 233–2385
www.ebls.org
E-mail: info@ebls.org

Rooms: Five bedrooms, two with private baths.

Rates: $290 to $410 per night, depending on the room. Cost
   includes boat transportation; hors d'oeuvres and

beverages upon arrival; a multicourse dinner with wines; and a hot breakfast.

Season: Year-round. Accommodations are available Thursday through Sunday night.

Restrictions: No smoking inside the buildings. No pets. Minimum age for overnight guests is eighteen years unless special arrangements are made.

Reservations: Prepaid reservations are required and are accepted by phone or e-mail. Visa, MasterCard, American Express and Discover cards and personal checks are accepted. Confirmation is made only upon receipt of payment.

There is a $30 cancellation fee; guests may be responsible for the entire cost if the room cannot be rebooked.

Check-in/out: Pickup time is 4:00 P.M. in front of the Galley Cafe at the Point San Pablo Yacht Harbor. Guests check-out and return to the mainland by 11:00 A.M.

Other features: Weddings and corporate retreats are available. There is a small gift shop at the lighthouse.

Other information: Dress is casual; keep luggage to a minimum. The weather is unpredictable; a jacket or sweater may be needed.

Water is in short supply. Showers are available only for guests staying more than one night.

Infrequently, the weather may be too rough to allow safe crossing, requiring cancellation, with full refund, on very short notice.

Directions: From Marin cross the Richmond–San Rafael Bridge. There is no Point Molate exit eastbound, so you need to backtrack. Take the first exit past the toll plaza (Richmond Parkway), cross under the freeway, then take the right on-ramp for I–580 west, heading back toward the bridge. Just before the toll plaza, take the Point Molate exit.

From East Bay, take I–80 (either direction) to the San Rafael exit, then take I–580 west toward the Richmond–San Rafael Bridge. Just before the toll plaza, take the Point Molate exit. Follow signs to the Point San Pablo Yacht Harbor.

THINGS TO DO

Nearly every spot on the island, including all of the rooms in the lighthouse, offers spectacular views. Guests often spend their time just watching the parade of sailboats and giant tankers that pass very close to the island.

Bring a book to read, a camera to document your stay, and binoculars to observe sea life and the maritime activity around the bay. Guests can fish from the island, but they must bring their own license, gear, and bait. The keepers provide a tour of the island, including history, restoration efforts, and, when functioning, a demonstration of the old diaphone fog signal.

 Pigeon Point Light Station
Pescadero, California

The lighthouse at Pigeon Point is named for a shipwreck. The clipper ship *Carrier Pigeon* was sailing from Boston to San Francisco with 1,300 tons of cargo when it ran aground on June 6, 1853, just short of its destination. Although the ship was lost, the crew was saved. The point of land was renamed Pigeon Point in memory of the ship.

Constructed of reinforced brick, the Pigeon Point Lighthouse is a classic American seacoast light tower, the tallest in California. The tower and an oil bunker are the only remaining original structures, which were built in 1872. The second fog signal building, built in 1902, is still in use for various hostel and park activities.

The tower houses a first-order Fresnel lens, the largest size used in American lighthouses. The light was originally fueled by lard oil, and later by kerosene. When it was electrified in the late 1920s, the 1,000-watt electric light bulb increased the light to 680,000 candlepower, which could be seen for 20 miles. The Fresnel lens, standing 16 feet tall, 6 feet in diameter, and weighing 8,000 pounds, is still in the tower, but it is only lit on special occasions. A 24-inch automated beacon was installed in 1972.

In December 2001 a portion of the tower fell off, resulting in the closing of the structure to visitors. The lighthouse tower may be viewed from the grounds, and hostel guides provide tours of the grounds for guests and visitors. The state park offers guided history walks between 10:00 A.M. and 4:00 P.M. Friday through Sunday. For the updated status of the tower and a tour schedule, call the California State Park hotline at (650) 879–2120.

STAYING THERE

The Pigeon Point Light Station guards a section of California coastline where many ships splintered on the rocks during the nineteenth-century. Today, the lighthouse welcomes visitors and provides a starting point for exploring a beautiful slice of coastal California.

The 115-foot lighthouse tower is perched on a 35-foot promontory above the Pacific Ocean along California's central coast about 50 miles south of San Francisco. It is hard to believe you are only a short drive from Silicon Valley.

The beachfront setting for the lighthouse could easily command outrageous rental fees, but as part of Hostelling International, the Pigeon Point Light Station offers budget accommodations to go along with an incredible view. The lodging experience is not up to the standards of some of the finer lighthouse B&Bs, but Pigeon Point provides an affordable, shared lighthouse lodging experience at one of California's most spectacular lighthouses.

In 1960 the Coast Guard built four three-bedroom houses next to the tower for use by Coast Guard personnel. Today, these structures offer overnight lodging for couples, families, small groups, and individuals. The lodging is dormitory style, with separate male and female bunk rooms, separate bunk rooms for families, shared bathrooms with showers, and access to fully equipped kitchens and living rooms.

The Pigeon Point Light Station Hostel is operated by the Golden Gate Council of Hostelling International–American Youth Hostels, a nonprofit membership organization, with cooperation from the California Department of Parks and Recreation and the United States Coast Guard. To help maintain the low-cost housing, the hostel asks guests to clean up after themselves and to volunteer to perform light chores around the houses.

Pigeon Point Light Station Hostel

210 Pigeon Point Road

Highway One

Pescadero, California 94060

(650) 879–0633

Fax: (650) 879–9120

www.norcalhostels.org/pigeonpointlighthouse

Rooms: Four houses provide accommodations for up to fifty-

The 115-foot tower at California's Pigeon Point Light Station is one of the tallest along the West Coast.

two guests of all ages. Each house has three male or female bunk rooms that accommodate up to six people. Private, separate bunk rooms may be reserved for families and couples at an extra cost. Guests share bathrooms with hot showers, fully equipped kitchens, and living rooms.

Rates: $15.00 per night for members of Hostelling International; $18.00 for nonmembers; $10.00 for children under twelve. There is a $1.00 per person linen rental fee.

Season: Year-round.

Restrictions: Alcohol is prohibited. No smoking is permitted inside the hostel buildings.

Reservations: Reservations are accepted by phone or mail with a credit card; Visa and MasterCard are accepted.
   For information about group rates, reservations, cancellations, and refunds, call the hostel between 7:30 and 9:30 A.M. and 5:30 and 9:30 P.M.
   Reservations are essential between January and September and on weekends.

Check-in/out: Check-in is from 4:30 to 9:30 P.M.; check-out and chores must be completed by 10:00 A.M.

Other features: School groups and religious, professional, or social organizations are welcome at all northern California hostels. Some hostels provide meeting facilities and educational or recreational programs for groups. Call the hostel in advance for further information about group facilities and reservation procedures. Meeting space and a private leader's room are available at Pigeon Point Lighthouse Hostel.

Other information: The weather in this area can be very changeable. Layered clothing is recommended, as is a rain jacket.

Directions: The lighthouse is located on California Highway 1, 50 miles south of San Francisco. It is about 20 miles south of Half Moon Bay and 27 miles north of Santa Cruz. It is hard to miss the 115-foot tower as you drive down the highway.

THINGS TO DO

The coastal areas surrounding the Pigeon Point Light Station are rich with sea life. Seals and whales can often be seen from shore. The boardwalk behind the Fog Signal Building is an especially good place to watch for gray whales during their annual migration. The peak viewing season for whales at Pigeon Point is March through May. The rocky reefs within walking distance of the lighthouse contain tidal pools with a rich diversity of plant and animal life.

Nearby **Pescadero State Beach** has a wide beach backed by sand dunes and saltwater ponds. It is described as one of the California coast's most scenic beaches. **Butano State Park** provides a change of pace from the beach with its 2,700 acres featuring a deep redwood forest. A short drive south on California Highway 1, the **Ano Nuevo State Reserve** is one of California's most spectacular coastal parks. From mid-December through March, the reserve is the breeding home of giant elephant seals.

 # Point Arena Lighthouse
Point Arena, California

The original Point Arena Lighthouse began operation in 1870. The lighthouse was placed at the end of a narrow peninsula to warn ships away from this stretch of inhospitable coastline.

The San Andreas Fault runs right under the Point Arena Lighthouse, plunging into the sea just north of the tower. The devastating San Francisco earthquake of 1906 severely damaged the original brick and mortar light tower, and a new reinforced concrete tower replaced it. The original ornate keepers' residence was also damaged beyond repair. Of the original structures only the wood-framed Fog Signal Building survived.

Because the government wanted the new lighthouse to be more earthquake proof, the 115-foot monolith was one of the first steel-reinforced concrete lighthouses in the United States. The iron spiral stairs and the lens room from the original light were used in the new tower. The original residence was replaced with four new houses. The new lighthouse began operation in 1908.

The Coast Guard automated the lighthouse in 1977, and it was not accessible to the public for several years. In 1982 a nonprofit corporation, the Point Arena Lighthouse Keepers, Inc., was formed to preserve the light station and keep it open to the public. The maintenance and development of the Point Arena Light Station are funded by admission fees, memberships, and lodging fees, with no tax dollars needed.

The lighthouse and museum are open to the public for tours every day except Thanksgiving, Christmas, and weekdays in December and January. A modest fee is required for entry. Tours are conducted by professional docents.

The museum, located in the Fog Signal Building, includes displays of historical equipment and photos, Coast Guard and shipwreck artifacts and charts, geographical maps and information on the area, and examples of local plants, birds, and whales. The work of local artists and photographers is also displayed.

STAYING THERE

The Point Arena Lighthouse and Museum are located on a magnificent peninsula with fantastic scenery. The experience of staying at the Point Arena Lighthouse is like vacationing at a nice family cottage at the beach, with the added attraction of the history and ambience of a working light station. Views from the lighthouse tower and the keepers' houses offer a dramatic perspective on this fabulous section of California coastline.

Part of the joy of this particular lighthouse lodging is getting to the location. The drive north from San Francisco along Highway 1 takes about three hours, if you don't bother to stop at the dozens of wonderful little towns, beaches, state parks, and other scenic distractions.

Neither the lighthouse tower nor the keepers' dwellings at Point Arena are the original structures. Those were destroyed by an earthquake. In the early 1960s the existing keepers' housing was razed, and four new homes were built to house coastguardsmen and their families assigned to the lighthouse.

The Point Arena Lighthouse is located on a beautiful stretch of California's scenic and rugged coastline.

Three of the keepers' homes have been renovated and are available to the public as vacation lodging. Each fully furnished home comprises approximately 1,400 square feet, with three bedrooms, two bathrooms, and a fully equipped kitchen and dining area. Each house has a large wood-burning stove, satellite TV, VCR, and great ocean views. A picnic table, lawn chairs, and barbecue grill are adjacent to each house.

Point Arena Lighthouse Keepers, Inc.

Attn: Reservations

P.O. Box 11

45500 Lighthouse Road

Point Arena, California 95468

(877) 725–4448 (24 hours) or (707) 882–2777

Fax: (707) 882–2111

www.pointarenalighthouse.com

E-mail: palight@mcn.org

Rooms: Three houses, each with three bedrooms and two private baths, and a full kitchen stocked with all cooking and dining utensils and appliances. Each house accommodates up to six people, including children, and includes one queen, one double, and two twin beds.

Rates: Rates vary by season and night of the week: Summer, May 16 through September 30, $155 per night Sunday through Thursday, $170 per night Friday and Saturday. Winter, October 1 through May 15, $140 per night Sunday through Thursday, $155 per night Friday and Saturday. A two-night minimum stay is required (one-night reservations are subject to availability). There is a three-night minimum stay for holidays. Discounts are offered on stays of seven or more days, not including holidays. Discounts are also offered for members of Point Arena Lighthouse Keepers, the Lighthouse Preservation Society, and the U.S. Lighthouse Society (holidays excluded).

Season: Year-round.

Restrictions: No smoking. No pets.

Reservations: Reservations are accepted up to six months in advance. Rooms often fill up quickly, especially on weekends, holidays, and during the summer and fall. A $100 deposit is taken at the time the reservation is made. If paying by check, the deposit must be received at least three weeks in advance of stay in order to secure the reservation. MasterCard, Visa, Diners Club, and Carte Blanche are also accepted. Ten percent of the deposit is charged for cancellations up to twenty-one days in advance of the stay. The entire deposit is charged for late cancellations.

Check-in/out: Check-in is after 3:00 P.M.; check-out is 11:00 A.M.

Other features: A beautiful gazebo located on the bluff behind the homes, the Fog Signal Building, and the tower itself can be reserved for weddings and other special occasions.

Other information: Due to limited water supply, guests are asked to provide their own sheets, pillow cases, and towels. If that is not possible because of travel arrangements, a setup of two bath towel sets, two pillow cases, and sheets can be provided for an additional fee.

Directions: The Point Arena Lighthouse is 135 miles north of San Francisco on the California coast in Mendocino County. From Point Arena, drive 1 mile north on California Highway 1, then 2 miles west on Lighthouse Road.

THINGS TO DO

The **Point Arena Lighthouse** is one of the best spots along the northern California coastline to view gray whales. Whales can usually be seen between December and April in most years.

There are a number of excellent beaches nearby, including **Manchester State Beach,** which offers 5 miles of sandy solitude. The **Point Arena Municipal Pier** allows fishing from the pier without a license. The pier also offers deep-sea fishing, boating access, shops, and restaurants.

The city of **Point Arena** has many shops, galleries, restaurants, a library, churches, and other services. **Gualala,** 16 miles south of the lighthouse, has shops, restaurants, galleries, campgrounds, beaches, churches, medical facilities, and other services.

Point Montara Lighthouse
Montara, California

After several shipwrecks in the mid-1800s, a fog signal was placed at Point Montara in 1872 to help ships negotiate the "thick weather" along the coast as they approached the entrance to San Francisco Bay. In 1900 a light tower was added at the site.

The first light was a red-lens lantern hung on a post. In 1912 a fourth-order Fresnel lens was installed on a skeleton tower, and the light was electrified in 1919. The Fresnel lens was moved to the current 30-foot tall cast-iron tower when it was built in 1928. The tower sits on a cliff 70 feet above the ocean.

The lighthouse served as a lookout for the Coast Guard during World War II, with several military units stationed nearby. The Coast Guard operated the station until 1970 when it was automated. Today, a small modern optic has replaced the original Fresnel lens, and an offshore signal has replaced the fog signal.

STAYING THERE

Like the Pigeon Point Light Station, Point Montara Lighthouse is operated as a hostel, which allows travelers on a limited budget to enjoy an overnight lighthouse experience. Both sites are managed by the Golden Gate Council of Hostelling International–American Youth Hostels, a worldwide network of low cost travel accommodations.

Hostels originated in Europe to provide travelers of all ages with an inexpensive, friendly atmosphere to spend the night. There are nearly 200 Hostelling International locations in the United States but few, in all likelihood, that offer an experience as unique as staying in a lighthouse.

Point Montara offers dorm-style family accommodations, with several kitchens, laundry, and telephone access available. "It is a nice shared experience for everyone," says Rich Lilley, the manager at the Point Montara Lighthouse since 1980. "It's just an exciting place to be." Guests provide their own linens and clean up after themselves. This self-help system allows hostels to be inexpensive and creates a friendly, cooperative spirit.

Point Montara Lighthouse Hostel

P.O. Box 737
16th Street at Highway 1
Montara, California 94037
(650) 728–7177
Telephone Tree Reservation System: (800) 909–4776, #64

Fax: (650) 728–7177

www.norcalhostels.org/pointmontaralighthouse. html

E-mail: himontara@norcalhostels.org

Rooms: Forty-five beds; lodging is bunk-bed-style, with five
private rooms available for an additional charge. Self-
service kitchen, meeting room, baggage storage, laundry,
and an information desk are available on-site. Wheelchair accessible.

Rates: $13–15 per person per night.

Season: Year-round.

Restrictions: Limited on-site parking. No pets. Smoking and
alcohol are prohibited.

Reservations: Reservations are essential between April and
September. Reservations are accepted by phone, fax, or
mail with a credit card. MasterCard and Visa are accepted. Phones are staffed from 7:30 to 9:30 A.M. and 5:00 to
9:30 P.M.

Check-in/out: Check-in is between 4:30 and 9:30 P.M.; check-
out is by 10:00 A.M.

Other features: Groups are welcome; day use of facilities by
groups is available by reservation.

Directions: Point Montara is located on California Highway 1,
25 miles south of San Francisco between Montara and
Moss Beach. Less than a half mile south of the town of
Montara, watch for the hostel sign, and turn onto a dirt
driveway. The lighthouse is visible from the road.

THINGS TO DO

Point Montara Lighthouse serves as a gateway to explore the
beautiful and rugged California coastline. Nearby is the
James Fitzgerald Marine Reserve, a 4-mile stretch of tidal
pools full of starfish, crabs, mussels, abalone, and sea
anemones. There are also several excellent beaches for
swimming, surfing, jogging, horseback riding, windsurfing,
and other outdoor activities. Whale watching is another
favorite activity during the annual migration of the gray
whales between November and April. There is easy access
for cycling along the shore on the **Bikecentennial
California Coast Bicycle Route.**

Heceta Head Lighthouse
Yachats, Oregon

The Heceta Head Lighthouse, completed in 1894, was one of the last to be built on the Oregon coast. The area was thought to be too rugged for construction of a light tower. Getting materials to the remote headland, hauling them up the cliffs to the site, and building the station took more than two years. The cost was more than $180,000, a tremendous sum at the time.

The Heceta Head Lighthouse was automated in July 1963. Heceta Head's first-order Fresnel lens is still in operation, creating one of the brightest lights along the Oregon coast. It shines an amazing 21 miles out to sea.

The 56-foot-tall lighthouse tower is a five-minute walk from the keeper's house. Guests are given flashlights so they can walk up to the base of the tower at night to see the spectacular lens in operation, an experience described as "magical."

Tours of the lighthouse tower are provided on a seasonal basis by the Oregon State Parks. For information about tours, call Honeyman State Park at (541) 997–3851.

STAYING THERE

The lighthouse at Heceta Head overlooks a breathtaking expanse of jagged rock, churning surf, and blue ocean. It is said to be the most photographed lighthouse in the United States. The tower and keeper's house stand on a cliff 205 feet above the sea, providing remarkable views of the coastline.

The Heceta Light Station Bed and Breakfast houses guests in the original light keeper's house. The site is owned by the U.S. Forest Service, but the B&B is operated by Michelle Korgan and Steven Bursey. Michelle is the daughter of Mike and Carol Korgan, who first started the B&B in 1995.

The Queen Anne–style keeper's house has six guest rooms, each individually decorated with period furniture and all with excellent views. Four of the rooms have private baths; two rooms share a bathroom. One guest we interviewed for the *Staying at a Lighthouse* TV program summed it up best: "From our bedroom window we see right down the coast, and it's just absolutely the most incredible view of the coastline, with the waves lapping up against the rocks."

Wooden, handcrafted, spiral staircases lead to the second-floor bedrooms. The romantic Queen Anne Room has a glamorous four-poster queen-size bed with elegant Austrian

sheers and a Victorian chaise longue. From the bathroom of
the Lightkeeper's Room, you can enjoy a magnificent view
of the lighthouse and ocean while soaking in the elegant
claw-foot tub. The beam from the Fresnel lens is visible all
night from the comfort of your queen-size bed.

Breakfast is served in two elegantly decorated dining
rooms. Guests relax in two parlors, each with its own fireplace and excellent view of the ocean. There is also a large
porch with comfortable chairs that offer unobstructed ocean
views. A large selection of books and games is available, and
guests have access to a kitchen for their use.

Michelle has maintained her parents' tradition of a
seven-course gourmet breakfast. She likes to keep the actual
menu a secret; it changes depending on what ingredients are
fresh and available.

The bed-and-breakfast operates a gift shop and an interpretive center, which offers public tours of the keeper's
house during the day. Tours are available between noon and
5:00 P.M. Thursday through Monday from Memorial Day to
Labor Day.

The interpretive program and the operation, maintenance, and repairs of the keeper's house are funded entirely
by lodging fees, donations, and proceeds from the gift shop.
The most recent renovations restored a guest room and
installed a sprinkler and fire-detection system.

The Heceta Light Station Bed and Breakfast

92072 Highway 101 South

Yachats, Oregon 97498

(541) 547-3696

www.hecetalighthouse.com

E-mail: keepers@hecetalighthouse.com

Rooms: Six rooms, four with private bath.

Rates: $135 to $220 per night, double occupancy; includes
breakfast. Most of the year, a minimum two-night stay
is required for Saturday bookings.

Season: Year-round.

Restrictions: No smoking, no pets, no children under the age
of ten. Limited wheelchair accessibility; call for information.

Reservations: Prepaid reservations are required. Visa and
MasterCard are accepted. There is a fee to cancel or

The Heceta Head Light Station B&B provides comfortable accommodations at one of the most beautiful lighthouse locations in the United States.

change your reservation. For the summer months it is usually necessary to make reservations two to four months in advance. During the slower winter months, only a week or two advance notice is usually necessary. Reservations are accepted by phone. Business hours are limited, so it is best to leave a daytime phone number and the dates you are interested in visiting. Although reservations are not accepted by e-mail, if you e-mail them a daytime phone number they will return the call as soon as possible.

Check-in/out: Check-in is between 3:00 and 5:00 P.M. (let them know if you'll be arriving later); check-out is by 10:30 A.M.

Other features: Special events such as weddings, corporate retreats, workshops, and family reunions can be held at the keeper's house. Each Christmas, the keeper's house is decorated inside and out, and different holiday events are held each night at no charge.

Directions: The Heceta Light Station Bed and Breakfast is halfway between the central Oregon coast towns of Florence and Yachats on US 101. From Portland driving time is between three and four hours, depending on the route you choose. The most direct route to travel is down I–5. However, the trip down scenic California Highway 101 is worth the extra time because it offers many places to stop and experience the Oregon coast.

THINGS TO DO

Beachcombing, exploring tidal pools, bird watching, and whale watching are all within a few minutes' walk of the keeper's house. The best time to spot whales is between March and July, as they head north, and in December as they head south.

There are several other Oregon lighthouses within driving distance of Heceta Head. An hour north, near Newport, are the **Yaquina Head Lighthouse** and the **Yaquina Bay Lighthouse.** Newport is also home to the **Oregon Coast Aquarium.** An hour south is the **Umpqua River Lighthouse.** Another hour's drive south is the **Cape Arago Lighthouse,** near Coos Bay, the **Coquille River Lighthouse,** and the **Cape Blanco Lighthouse.**

The nearby Oregon coastal towns of **Florence** and **Yachats** offer visitors plenty of lunch and dinner options. The **Oregon Dunes National Recreational Area,** just south of Florence, is one of the few spots along the Oregon coast not protected by rocky headlands. The dunes stretch for more than 40 miles, and walking or riding a dune buggy through them provides an almost otherworldly experience.

 ## Browns Point Lighthouse
Browns Point, Washington

In 1887, two years before Washington became a state, a fixed white lantern was placed on a pole about 12 feet above sea level on Point Brown. A "keeper" rowed out once a week to clean and refuel the lantern. The light marked an important turning point for ships entering Commencement Bay and the port at Tacoma.

The Lighthouse Service built a wooden tower and keeper's residence at Browns Point in 1903 at a cost of around $3,000. In 1920 electricity was installed, increasing the effectiveness of the light. In 1933 the current concrete art deco tower with a diaphragm fog signal was built. The lighthouse was automated in 1963.

Today the property is a public park owned by the Coast Guard, which maintains the light. The Metropolitan Park District of Tacoma maintains the rest of the park and buildings, and the Points Northwest Historical Society assists in the stewardship efforts.

The first lighthouse keeper was, coincidentally, named Oscar Brown. At the one keeper station, Brown was on call twenty-four hours a day. He served at the Browns Point Lighthouse for thirty-six years, retiring at the age of seventy-two. Brown had served a total of fifty-one years as a lighthouse keeper in Washington state.

In addition to the tower and keeper's cottage, there are an oil house, pump house, and boathouse. The Boathouse houses a 16½-foot replica of a Coast Guard surf boat. The 1950s crew quarters building is now a history center.

STAYING THERE

In a 1913 newspaper article, visitors to the Browns Point Lighthouse were quoted as telling the keeper "what a great summer home" the lighthouse would make. The visitors were clearly taken by the pastoral setting and the ninety-degree views of the Puget Sound offered at the lighthouse. The keeper told the reporter, "His life is not the summer vacation some persons think it is."

Today, the Browns Point Lighthouse invites guests to experience the beauty and serenity of being a lighthouse keeper, without quite as much work and time commitment. Guests become lighthouse keepers for a one-week tour of duty when they stay in the keeper's cottage. Duties include such things as conducting tours of the lighthouse grounds and facilities, doing light daily maintenance, and raising the flag each morning.

The quaint keeper's cottage sits in a grassy park near the unincorporated town of Browns Point. It has been restored with period furnishings from the early 1900s. The main floor has a comfortable parlor and dining room. The kitchen has been modernized and includes a dishwasher, microwave, stove and oven, refrigerator, coffeemaker, dishes, and pots and pans.

The main-floor bedroom, which was the keeper's sitting room, has a TV and VCR and a queen size hideaway bed. The bathroom has the original claw-foot bathtub and a shower. The spacious upstairs master bedroom has a queen-size bed and a large closet. The "bunk room" has a double antique brass bed and a set of twin beds. There are a washer and dryer in the basement.

Browns Point Lighthouse

Points Northeast Historical Society

6622 Eastside Drive N.E.

PMB 135

Browns Point, Washington 98422

(253) 927–2536

www.pointsnortheast.org

E-mail: lighthouse@southsound.com

Rooms: Three bedrooms, shared bathroom. Houses a minimum of two adults and a maximum of six people. Children are welcome.

Rates: $500 per week from October 29 to April 29, $600 per week from April 30 to October 28, plus a $20 family membership. A $200 refundable damage/cleaning deposit is required.

Season: Year-round.

Restrictions: No smoking in the buildings. No drugs or alcohol or firearms on the premises. No pets.

Reservations: Accepted by phone or mail. You must complete a reservation and membership application and pay all fees at least sixty days prior to your date of arrival. Tours of duty are reserved on a first-come first-served basis. When Points Northeast Historical Society has received your membership fee, damage/cleaning deposit, and rental fee, you will be issued a confirmation letter. Cancellations must be received sixty days prior to your tour of duty in order to receive a refund.

Check-in/out: Tour of duty is Sunday to Sunday. Check-in is 2:00 P.M.; check-out is 11:00 A.M.

Other information: Bedding and towels are provided. Guest are ask to launder and fold them at the end of their stay.

Directions: From I–5, take exit 142B. Go west on South 348th Street for 6.8 miles. At the stop sign at the end of Slayden Road, turn right onto Marine View Drive. Take the first left onto Le Lou Wa Place NE (there is a shopping center on the right). Continue 0.3 mile, turn right on La Hal Da Avenue NW, and drive another 0.3 mile. Take a sharp left onto Tulalip Street NE, and go a half block through the gate to the lighthouse.

THINGS TO DO

Browns Point is a ten-minute drive from **Tacoma** and a thirty-minute drive from **Seattle.**

The community of **Browns Point** has a grocery store, an espresso shop, a pizza shop, a hardware store, a small shopping center, and several restaurants.

Visitors to Browns Point Lighthouse can explore the pastoral beauty and natural wonders of **Puget Sound.** Wedged between the foothills of two great mountain ranges, Puget Sound extends 80 miles from the Strait of Juan de Fuca to Olympia. It reaches depths of 900 feet and is an important transportation hub for Washington's lumber industry.

New Dungeness Lighthouse
Sequim, Washington

The Strait of Juan de Fuca connects the Pacific Ocean to the inland passages of the Puget Sound, British Columbia, and Southeast Alaska. Four lighthouses were built along the northern coastline of Washington to help guide ships through the strait. Only two of the lighthouses survived, and only New Dungeness Lighthouse is open to the public.

The maritime hazard here is created by the New Dungeness Spit, a low, narrow, sandy strip of land that stretches for 5½ miles into the strait and is barely visible from the sea. When the lighthouse was completed in 1857, it was near the end of the spit. Today, the lighthouse sits a half mile from the tip, the result of sand constantly moving with the currents and tides.

The lighthouse tower rises up from the center of the keeper's house. In 1904 a second dwelling was completed to accommodate assistant keepers and their families.

The original brick tower was 100 feet high, the third tallest in Washington state. When cracks developed in the tower in the 1920s, it was reduced to only 63 feet. The original bricks that were removed can still be found scattered around the site.

The lighthouse has had several Fresnel lenses. The most recent one, a fourth-order lens, was removed in 1976. Today, a modern rotating beacon serves local fishermen and ships at sea.

When the Coast Guard removed the last keeper in March 1994, the future of the lighthouse was in jeopardy. The Coast Guard planned to maintain the light but board up the buildings. That's when the New Dungeness Chapter of the United States Lighthouse Society was formed. Because the transfer of the light station to a local group occurred so close to when the Coast Guard pulled out, New Dungeness Lighthouse avoided the years of neglect and disrepair that befell so many U.S. lighthouses. The chapter has maintained the lighthouse ever since.

STAYING THERE

There are a few lighthouses in the United States that allow guests to serve as part-time lighthouse keepers. These places don't provide the service, food, and other amenities of a lighthouse B&B, but they do offer a unique opportunity to discover a little of what it was like to be an actual lighthouse keeper.

Since September 1994, volunteer keepers have continuously staffed the New Dungeness Lighthouse in Washington. Volunteer keepers stay in the keeper's quarters built in 1904, the newer of the two structures at New Dungeness. It is a three-bedroom, two-bathroom house that accommodates up to seven people. The house has a full kitchen, and bedding is provided. Guests must bring their own food. An artesian well provides fresh water to the light station.

Typically, two or three couples go out to the lighthouse on Friday night or Saturday morning for a weeklong stay.

Guests at the New Dungeness Lighthouse in Washington state are asked to perform light chores to help maintain the facility.

Couples with children are welcome. The timing of the trip depends on the tide. Because there are no roads to the light-house, transportation is along the beach in a four-wheel-drive vehicle. In winter the low tides occur only at night, making for some interesting trips at very odd hours.

During the week volunteer keepers perform light main-tenance, cleaning, and minor repair work around the house and the grounds. All persons staying at the light station view an orientation and safety video, sign a release, and pay a fee.

Volunteer keepers also provide tours for visitors. Despite its remote location and lack of access, the lighthouse gets an amazing number of visitors each year. Most walk to the lighthouse, but others come by boat, kayak, and occasionally on horseback. The waters around the spit are popular with local fishermen.

To stay at the lighthouse and serve as a volunteer keeper, you must be a member of both the U.S. Lighthouse Society and the New Dungeness Chapter. One check enrolls you in both organizations. Annual dues are $50 per household for U.S. residents. A membership application is available at www.dungeness.com/lighthouse.

If you are interested in the type of experience offered at the New Dungeness Light Station, you might want to join right away to get on the list of volunteer keepers. The lighthouse is usually booked more than a year and a half ahead, although there are occasional last-minute openings. The Web site provides available dates.

Those who pay for the privilege of working at the lighthouse don't seem to mind. "Our members are delighted to pay the modest sum that we charge them to stay out here," says one of the chapter's founders in an interview for the *Legendary Lighthouses* TV series. "There are some who simply want to be out here for a week of solitude, there are others who love to work on projects, there are others who just really get a kick out of guiding visitors around. There is something for every kind of personality out here."

New Dungeness Lighthouse

Membership and Scheduling Services

P.O. Box 1283

Sequim, Washington 98382

(360) 683–6638

Fax: (360) 683–1251

www.ndlightstation.com

E-mail: scheduling@ndlightstation.com

Rooms: Three-bedroom, two-bath house accommodates up to seven people.

Rates: Volunteer keepers must pay a fee of $250 per adult and $100 per child (under eighteen) to stay at the lighthouse. The fee is used to maintain and renovate the light station, keepers' quarters, and other buildings.

Season: Year-round.

Restrictions: No smoking is allowed inside any of the lighthouse buildings. No pets. Children six years and older are welcome but must be strictly supervised. The job of a volunteer keeper is a physical one and includes tours of the light tower (with its seventy-four steps), mowing the lawn, and generally keeping the station clean and safe. The remote location may not be suitable for the physically challenged.

Reservations: Full information on how to schedule a stay at the light station will be sent to you once your membership application is processed. Vacancies sometimes become available on short notice; you can indicate on your application if you would be interested in covering such a vacancy.

Other features: Membership includes the member newsletter, *Foghorn,* which lists scheduling opportunities and other information about the light station.

Other information: The lighthouse is open to the public from 9:00 A.M. to 4:00 P.M., seven days a week.

Check-in/out: Varies depending on tides.

Directions: Take US 101 west of Sequim, turn north, and follow signs to the Dungeness National Wildlife Refuge. Access to the lighthouse is by boat or an 8-mile round-trip hike along the scenic Dungeness Spit.

T H I N G S   T O   D O

"The location is the attraction," says longtime member Barry Dove. "It's isolated but accessible." Shipping lanes that pass right by the lighthouse provide an occasional diversion. Wildlife is abundant, including bald eagles, seals, sea lions, hawks, deer, and many types of birds. The scenery includes the Olympic Mountains to the south, the Cascades to the east, the San Juan Islands to the north, and Vancouver island to the northwest.

North Head Lighthouse
Ilwaco, Washington

The North Head Lighthouse was built in response to the large number of shipwrecks along the peninsula caused as vessels sailed north but could not yet see the Cape Disappointment Lighthouse. The 65-foot North Head tower sits on a rock base more than 190 feet above sea level.

The two keepers' dwellings served as home for a head keeper, two assistants, and their families. Keepers typically worked eight-hour shifts, with longer shifts common during storms. They carried kerosene up the sixty-four stairs to the lens room, trimmed wicks, cleaned the lens, and generally kept the entire facility spotlessly clean.

North Head is the windiest lighthouse location on the West Coast and the third windiest in the nation. Winds of 120 miles per hour have been recorded at the site. One story retold over the years is of a duck blown off course in 1932 that crashed through the lighthouse window and chipped the Fresnel lens. Another story tells of a keeper's wife who jumped to her death from the cliff, unable to bear the constant howling of the wind. Because of the turbulent seas where the Columbia River meets the ocean, the Coast Guard's rough-water lifesaving school is nearby. "The Columbia River bar is noted for some of the roughest sea conditions in the world," said one of the coastguardsmen we interviewed for the *Legendary Lighthouses* TV series. "In one direction you have waves coming in off thousands of miles of unobstructed water. In the other you have a powerful outgoing current. On a rough day you can have 15- to 20-foot breakers in this area."

STAYING THERE

The area where the Pacific Ocean and the mighty Columbia River meet has long been one of the most important yet hazardous locations for ships along the West Coast. Not only a gateway for early explorers and pioneers, it was also the popular water route to Portland and the inland West—but not without risk. The area around the Long Beach Peninsula of Washington is known as the "Graveyard of the Pacific."

Two lighthouses were built to help guide ships through the high waves and shifting sandbars. The Cape Disappointment Lighthouse, completed in 1856, directed mariners into the

The North Head Lighthouse sits high above the Pacific Ocean at what is considered one of the windiest lighthouse locations in the country.

mouth of the Columbia River. The North Head Lighthouse, built in 1898, guided ships approaching from farther north.

Today, the two keepers' houses at North Head Lighthouse serve as a great base from which to explore the scenic and natural wonders of Long Beach Peninsula. The lighthouse is part of Fort Canby State Park.

Guests stay in the two original residences used by keepers and their families. Both of the two-story Victorian-period houses offer breathtaking views of the mouth of the Columbia River and the Pacific Ocean.

Each three-bedroom house accommodates up to six people. Features include hardwood floors in the living room, dining room, and library, and a spacious kitchen with modern appliances and all cooking and dining utensils. Linens are provided. Guests must bring their own food.

The houses are located just inland from the North Head Lighthouse. Guests are invited to join regular tours of the lighthouse tower, which are offered by Fort Canby State Park.

North Head Lighthouse

Fort Canby State Park

P.O. Box 488

Ilwaco, Washington 98624

(360) 642–3078 or (800) 360–4240

TDD: (360) 753–2036

Fax: (360) 642–4216

www.fortcanby.org, www.parks.wa.gov

E-mail: info@fortcanby.org

Rooms: Two three-bedroom houses, each with two queen-size beds and two twin beds. Each house is similarly equipped with a dining room that seats six at a large table, and a kitchen that includes a range, microwave, coffeemaker, refrigerator, dishwasher, and all necessities. All linens and towels are provided.

Rates: $251.97 per night, per house. Depending on demand, off-season discounts are sometimes offered between October 1 and May 15.

Season: Year-round.

Reservations: Reservations are accepted by phone. Deposit of first and last days' rent is required. Visa, MasterCard, American Express, and Discover cards and personal checks are accepted. Reservations are generally taken nine months in advance and are recommended for weekends, holidays, and peak summer periods. The houses are rented by the day, week, or month. A minimum two-night stay is required; a minimum three-night stay is required on holidays.

Other features: The lighthouse grounds can be rented for weddings and other special events.

Other information: There is no TV reception at the houses. A television set with a VCR and an FM radio are available in each house. Call (360) 902–8844 for information and a free brochure about the heritage vacation housing opportunities available through Washington State Parks.

Directions: North Head Lighthouse is a good three-hour drive south of Seattle and about a ninety-minute drive from Portland. At exit 40 on I–5, take State Route 4 west to US 101 into the town of Ilwaco, and then follow signs to Fort Canby State Park. Markers inside the park point the way to the lighthouse.

THINGS TO DO

Fort Canby State Park is located at the base of the popular Long Beach Peninsula. Guests who stay at the keepers' houses can tour the park's historical coast, stroll along two sandy beaches, hike four nearby scenic trails through coastal forests and headlands, bike along the park's paved roads, and enjoy a variety of recreational activities. The **Lewis and Clark Interpretive Center** at Fort Canby provides a great deal of information about the expedition, including a timeline of the journey, excerpts from diaries, and mementos.

The first-order Fresnel lens used in the North Head Lighthouse is on display at **Fort Canby State Park Interpretive Center.** The **Cape Disappointment Lighthouse** is located south of North Head.

North Head is within easy reach of **Astoria,** Oregon. With its many fine, old homes, Astoria is a popular tourist destination. One attraction on the Astoria waterfront is the **Lightship Columbia,** which once helped guide vessels across the river's treacherous sandbar.

Big Bay Point Lighthouse
Big Bay, Michigan

The Big Bay Lighthouse went into operation in 1896. The light was built on a high, rocky point that marked an unlit area of the Lake Superior shoreline. The original lighthouse consisted of a two-story, 18-room brick duplex with a light tower rising from the center of the house.

The lighthouse was automated in 1941. For many years it served as an antiaircraft artillery training facility for the Army and National Guard. Large guns were installed on the cliffs to the east of the lighthouse.

In 1961 the lighthouse was sold to the first of several private owners. Each made improvements and additions to the lighthouse structures. In 1991 the current owners—John Gale and Jeff and Linda Gamble of Chicago—bought the lighthouse; Jeff and Linda live in the lighthouse and serve as full-time innkeepers.

STAYING THERE

A casual, secluded retreat awaits guests at the Big Bay Lighthouse Bed and Breakfast on the Upper Peninsula of Michigan. The lighthouse sits high atop a cliff jutting into the clear, deep waters of Lake Superior. The two-story brick building and its adjoining 60-foot-high square tower are located on more than forty acres of woods along a half mile of Lake Superior shoreline.

The fourteen-room inn has seven guest rooms with private baths, a common living room with a fireplace and library, as well as a sauna. The rooms vary slightly in size and location, but all have excellent views.

Each room is named for a former keeper, assistant keeper, or helper at the lighthouse. The large Keeper Defrain Room has a view of Lake Superior, a vaulted ceiling, and a gas fireplace. The Keeper Bergan Room has a first-floor view of Lake Superior, a gas Franklin stove, and a one-person thermo-massage tub and shower. The smaller Helper Brown and Helper Fleurey Rooms have views of the woods.

Guests can climb to the lighthouse lantern room, which is more than 100 feet above the lake surface. The vantage point provides views of fields and wildflowers, dense forests, the majestic Huron Mountains in the distance, and the ever

Sand Hills Lighthouse

Whitefish Point Lighthouse

Two Harbors Lighthouse

C A N

Lake Superior

MN

Duluth

■ Ironwood

Marquette

MI

Apostle Islands Lighthouses

Big Bay Point Lighthouse

Escanaba ■

WI

MI

Lake Michigan

■ Muskegon

Milwaukee ■

Chicago ■

IA

IL

IN

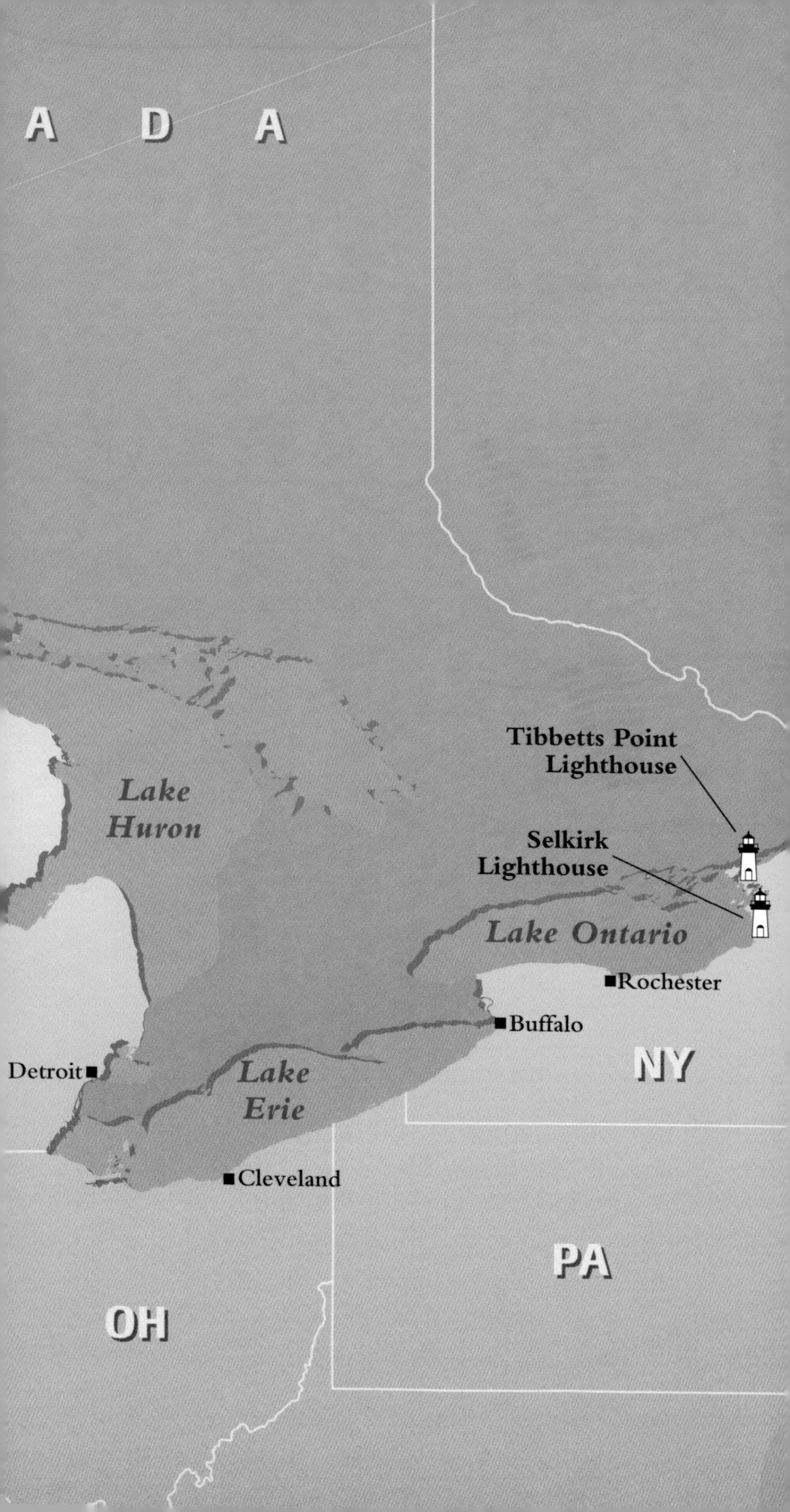

CANADA

Lake
Huron

Tibbetts Point
Lighthouse

Selkirk
Lighthouse

Lake Ontario

Rochester

Buffalo

NY

Detroit

Lake
Erie

Cleveland

OH

PA

changing Lake Superior. The inn offers something unique for a lighthouse B&B. A Massage Hut sits just below the lighthouse in a secluded wooded area. The sights and scents of the lake and woods add to the relaxation of the massage. In addition, arm, hand, face, and foot massages are offered right in the lighthouse. Special lighthouse spa packages are available between Memorial Day and October 15.

Big Bay Point Lighthouse Bed and Breakfast

3 Lighthouse Road

Big Bay, Michigan 49808

(906) 345–9957

www.bigbaylighthouse.com

E-mail: keepers@bigbaylighthouse.com

Rooms: Seven rooms, each with a private bath. Some baths are across the hall from the bedroom, but the inn provides robes.

Rates: Rates vary depending on the room and time of the year: Keeper Rooms are $183 from May 1 through October, and $160 from November 1 through April. Assistants Rooms are $143 from May 1 through October, and $125 from November 1 through April. Helper Rooms are $115–$123 from May 1 through October, and $99–$107 from November 1 through April. Price includes room, full breakfast, and use of the facilities. Lighthouse spa packages are available from Memorial Day through October 15. Rates are $344–$480 per night, based on double occupancy, and include lodging, dinner for two at the Thunder Bay Inn, breakfast both mornings, and a one-hour relaxation massage per person in the Massage Hut.

Season: The inn is closed from November 15 to December 26.

Restrictions: No pets. No smoking inside the buildings. No children under sixteen.

Reservations: Reservations are easiest by phone but can also be made by e-mail. A reservation request form is available on the Web site. A deposit by check equal to the first night's stay is required within fourteen days of making the reservation. Balance is due twenty-one days prior to arrival. No credit cards are accepted. A confirmation will be sent via U.S. mail.

A two-night minimum stay is required for Friday and Saturday from Memorial Day through October and between December 27 and January 1. A three-night stay is required for Labor Day.

With a minimum twenty-one-day notice, deposits are refunded with a $25 handling fee per room. Deposits are forfeited with less than twenty-one days' notice. Many rooms are booked well in advance, especially for holidays and weekend. The Web site has a reservation grid that displays the availability of rooms.

Check-in/out: Check-in is between 4:00 and 6:00 P.M., unless prior arrangements are made. Check out is 11:00 A.M.

Other features: Guests have use of the living room with fireplace, library with TV and VCR, and a sauna. Books, games, and a large selection of CDs and videotapes are available. Massages are available to guests, either in the lighthouse or in the Massage Hut, at an extra cost depending on the type of massage.

Other information: Each evening around 5:00 P.M. in the living room, there is a brief presentation about the history of the lighthouse.

Directions: The lighthouse is 26 miles north of Marquette in Michigan's Upper Peninsula. From Marquette take County Route 550 north into the town of Big Bay, then follow the lighthouse signs for 3½ miles to the inn.

THINGS TO DO

The town of **Big Bay,** with a population of 320, is filled with local culture. Its claim to fame is that is was the setting for Otto Preminger's classic film *Anatomy of a Murder.*

The town has grocery and convenience stores, a laundry, gift shops, restaurants, a restored train depot, and the **Thunder Bay Inn,** once owned by auto tycoon Henry Ford.

Boat and snowmobile rentals, a marina, and tour guides for wilderness waterfall and sunset kayak tours are offered. Downhill skiing, rock climbing, canoeing, mountain biking, and hiking are among the activities available. Marquette County has a variety of summer ethnic, arts, and music festivals, historic walking tours, a maritime museum, and numerous antiques shops.

Sand Hills Lighthouse
Ahmeek, Michigan

The Lighthouse Board lobbied for many years for a light-house along a section of the Lake Superior shoreline where eastbound ships made a turn off Sand Hills. The spot was not marked by a light, forcing ships to run blind at night. The Sawtooth Reef, located just off Sand Hills, sent many vessels to the bottom of Lake Superior, resulting in millions of dollars in losses.

By 1917 a temporary light and fog signal were erected at Five Mile Point while the lighthouse was being built. Because there were no roads to the tip of the peninsula, all of the materials for the lighthouse were brought in by barge. The lighthouse went into operation in 1919.

The Sand Hills Lighthouse had a relatively brief period of usage. It was only manned for twenty years and had only one head keeper, William R. Bennetts, who served at Sand Hills from 1919 to 1939. The light was automated in 1939 and eventually taken out of service in 1954.

In 1961 Detroit photographer and artist Bill Frabotta bought the lighthouse. He restored the fog signal building and used it as a summer cottage for thirty years. In 1995 Frabotta completed a three-year renovation of the entire lighthouse and opened it as a bed-and-breakfast inn.

STAYING THERE

The curved spit of land that juts into Lake Superior to form the Keweenaw Peninsula seems a perfect spot for a light-house stay. This remote outpost provides a sense of the isolation faced by many lighthouse keepers on the Great Lakes, along with a feeling of modern-day luxury that is hard to top.

Sand Hills, the largest lighthouse ever built on the Great Lakes, is considered the "last word" in lighthouse design and construction. The tower rises up seven floors in the center of the massive reinforced concrete keepers' dwelling. Inside are carved oak staircase railings, plaster medallions around the light fixtures, and antique Victorian furnishings. The walls of the parlor, which has a fireplace, are covered in floor-to-ceiling oak wainscoting.

"People are thrilled to stay at a lighthouse," says Bill Frabotta, owner and keeper of the Sand Hills Lighthouse Inn, "to hear the seagulls or the water and enjoy the majesty of Lake Superior. And sooner or later, they head for the tower." At more than 100 feet above lake level, few signs of civilization can be spotted from the lens room, adding to the isolation and serenity.

The Sand Hills Lighthouse Inn is beautifully situated on thirty-five acres of wooded land with 3,000 feet of Lake Superior shoreline. The inn has eight guest rooms, all with private baths and some with balconies, fireplaces, and canopied beds.

The Sir Laurence Olivier Room, complete with an autographed photo of the actor as Hamlet, was the head lightkeeper's bedroom. It features 94 yards of purple velvet, a king-size canopy bed, an antique marble fireplace, and a window that faces the lake and the sunset. The Northwest Balcony Room has French doors leading to a balcony where guests watch the sunset each evening. The room is one of two that has a whirlpool bath. The Southwest Quarters Room was used by the assistant keeper's family. It is decorated with an antique armoire, old hats, and antique walking sticks.

The giant Sand Hills Lighthouse sits along a remote stretch of Lake Superior.

The Common Room has comfortable leather sofas that are great for relaxing or enjoying a book, especially if someone is playing the nearby ninety-four-year-old grand piano. The sitting area at the bottom of the stairs that lead to the lens room in the tower is another popular gathering area for guests.

The recently renovated Barracks Building provides another place for guests to relax. The first building ever built on the site, it housed the construction crew that built the lighthouse. Elegantly restored with English woodwork, it has an antique pool table that gets lots of attention.

Guests can enjoy the sunrise from many spots on the property, including the rocky shore, the front porch, a private balcony, and the lighthouse tower. The smell of specially blended coffee fills the house, and guests enjoy a sumptuous breakfast served at 9:30 A.M. The breakfast menu includes Sand Hills traditions like Bill's Decadent French Toast and Merry Mary's Sunshine Soufflé.

Sand Hills Lighthouse Inn

Five Mile Point Road

P.O. Box 414

Ahmeek, Michigan 49901

(906) 337–1744

www.sandhillslighthouseinn.com

E-mail: frabotta@up.net

Rooms: Each of the eight rooms has a king- or queen-size bed and private bathroom. Two rooms have whirlpool bathtubs and a balcony overlooking Lake Superior. No TV or phones.

Rates: $125 to $185, includes full breakfast.

Season: Year-round.

Restrictions: No smoking. No pets.

Reservations: Reservations can be guaranteed with a one-night deposit by cash, check, or traveler's check. No credit cards are accepted. A two-night minimum stay is required from May through October and on weekends. Two weeks' notice is required to receive a full refund on cancellations.

Check-in/out: Check-in is 4:00 P.M.; check-out is noon.

Other features: Some rooms have whirlpool baths, air-conditioning. An elegant dessert is served each evening. Snacks and refreshments are available.

Other information: For guests who depart before the full breakfast service at 9:30 A.M., juice, coffee, and pastries are provided.

Directions: Sand Hills Lighthouse Inn is 25 miles northeast of Houghton on the Keweenaw Peninsula's north shore. Take US 41 north to the tiny village of Ahmeek; turn left at the first street. Follow the signs to Five Mile Point Road, and continue 8 miles to the lighthouse.

THINGS TO DO

The natural, isolated setting and the elegant accommodations of the Sand Hills Lighthouse Inn provide a perfect opportunity to enjoy the luxury of doing very little. The charm of the inn and the beauty of the surroundings are enough to fill the time for most visitors who stay at the lighthouse.

There are many attractions within thirty minutes of the lighthouse, including copper mine tours, museums, waterfalls, antiques shops, and other Michigan lighthouses.

Whitefish Point Lighthouse
Paradise, Michigan

Whitefish Point is the oldest active lighthouse on Lake Superior. The original stone lighthouse at Whitefish Point was built in 1848. In the closing days of the Civil War, President Abraham Lincoln ordered the construction of the present 80-foot-tall iron pile tower.

The unusual-looking metal structure has a central column supported by four heavily braced legs. This open design, sometimes called a steel skeleton, allows even the strongest winds to pass through the structure. The Whitefish Point Lighthouse has survived even the most destructive gales.

Ships that use this route haven't always been so lucky. Of the estimated 550 large vessels that have gone down in Lake Superior, about one-third have met their final end within the 100-mile stretch between Whitefish Point and Marquette, earning it the name Shipwreck Coast.

The Whitefish Point Lighthouse marks an area of Lake Superior known as the Shipwreck Coast.

The best-known shipwreck on the Great Lakes was the *Edmund Fitzgerald* in 1975. The sinking of the 729-foot freighter in a fierce storm on Lake Superior was turned into legend by Gordon Lightfoot's popular ballad "The Wreck of the Edmund Fitzgerald."

The shipwreck lies about 17 miles northwest of the Whitefish Point Light Station. The lighthouse, shipwreck museum, and lifesaving station are the best place to discover the history of this famous maritime disaster and learn more about the area of Lake Superior known as the Shipwreck Coast.

The night the *Edmund Fitzgerald* sank, the Whitefish Point Lighthouse was dark because the storm had knocked out electricity along the entire peninsula. It is unlikely, however, that the lighthouse failure had anything to do with the sinking. The ship never got close enough for its crew to see the light, even if it had been operating.

STAYING THERE

The accommodations available at Whitefish Point are not in the lighthouse or the keeper's quarters, but they offer no less of a historic maritime experience. Visitors who become members of the Great Lakes Shipwreck Historical Society can stay overnight at the restored 1923 U.S. Coast Guard Lifeboat Station Crew's Quarters located next to the Whitefish Point Lighthouse.

Each of the themed rooms has a private bath and entertainment center. Among the items on display throughout the Crew's Quarters are actual images capturing historic moments of lifesaving and Coast Guard personnel stationed at Whitefish Point. A continental breakfast is available each morning. Guests are responsible for all other meals.

Nearby, the 1861 lighthouse keeper's quarters have been restored to the original turn-of-the-twentieth-century appearance. The house contains many exhibits, artifacts, period furnishings, and descriptive panels that tell the stories of keepers and their families from the days of the U.S. Lighthouse Service and the U.S. Lifesaving Service. The last keeper was removed when the light station was automated in 1970.

Whitefish Point Lighthouse

Great Lakes Shipwreck Historical Society
18335 North Whitefish Point Road
Paradise, Michigan 49768

(888) 397–3747

Fax: (906) 497–3383

www.shipwreckmuseum.com

Rooms: Five private rooms, each with its own bathroom.

Rates: $150 per night, double occupancy. All linens are provided.

Season: Year-round.

Restrictions: No children under sixteen, Pets, smoking, and alcohol are prohibited.

Reservations: Reservations are accepted by phone. A credit card is required to hold the reservation. Visa, MasterCard, Discover, and American Express are accepted.

Check-in/out: Check-in is 2:00 P.M.; check-out is 11:00 A.M.

Other features: Data ports with full satellite technology are available in each room.

Other information: To be able to stay at the Lifesaving Station, you must first join the Great Lakes Shipwreck Coast Historical Society. Membership is $25 for individuals and $35 for families. Members also receive access to the entire complex and a 10 percent discount on items purchased at the gift shop and the on-line store.

Directions: The lighthouse is an eighty-minute drive from the Straits of Mackinaw. Take I–75 north to State Route 123 (exit 352), the Newberry/Tahquamenon Falls exit. Follow State Route 123 through Trout Lake all the way to Paradise. Turn north on Whitefish Point Road, and continue 11 miles to the Whitefish Point Light Station. From Sault Sainte Marie it's a seventy-five-minute drive to the lighthouse. Take I–75 south to State Route 28 west (exit 386). Turn north onto State Route 123 to Paradise, then continue north on Whitefish Point Road for 11 miles to the Whitefish Point Light Station.

THINGS TO DO

Interpreters provide guided tours of the keeper's home and the **Shipwreck Museum,** which presents 400 years of exploration, Great Lakes shipping, lifesaving heroism, and maritime history. The museum is full of maritime displays and artifacts. The memorial to the *Edmund Fitzgerald,* including the ship's bell recovered in 1995, may be viewed in the museum. Also on the grounds is the **Whitefish Point Bird Observatory,** hosting an interpretive center on Audubon Society programs, research, migration routes, and other information.

Two Harbors Lighthouse
Two Harbors, Minnesota

The Two Harbors Lighthouse sits on a point along the busy maritime highway between Agate and Burlington Bays. The structure went into operation in 1892 to aid the busy iron ore and other shipping traffic in the area.

The 49-foot-high tower is connected to the keeper's house. The tower itself is 12 feet square and three bricks thick, which provided some protection for the keeper and his family from the oil that was burned to light the lamps in the tower.

You'll pass several rooms as you climb the tower stairs. The first room is a bedroom used by the second assistant keeper. Next is the watch room, and just below the light is the cleaning room. On top is the lantern room, which houses the light.

The lighthouse originally had a fourth-order Fresnel lens, which is now on display at the Inland Sea Museum in Vermillion, Ohio. The historical society hopes to bring the classic lens back to Two Harbors someday. A modern beacon, installed in 1970, continues to operate today.

STAYING THERE

More than 350 miles long, 160 miles wide, and covering more than 31,000 square miles, Lake Superior is the world's largest freshwater lake. The Great Lakes make up one of America's most important transportation corridors. Freighters from around the world, many of them several football fields long, operate in these waters. Over the years dozens of ships have sunk in the often stormy, treacherous waters. The seemingly endless coastline of the Great Lakes is marked by many lighthouses, outposts along some of the most isolated shoreline in the country.

The Two Harbors Lighthouse on the western edge of Lake Superior helped guide huge iron ore ships around the Great Lakes. The square redbrick tower attached to the keeper's house directed ships into the busy harbor at Agate Bay. Two Harbors is the oldest continuously operated lighthouse in Minnesota.

A stay at the picturesque Two Harbors Lighthouse combines a unique lighthouse accommodation with a sense of history and a chance to participate in the preservation of an important aspect of America's maritime history. The lighthouse inn, operated by the Lake County Historical Society, looks as much like an old redbrick schoolhouse as it does a lighthouse, except for the lens room atop the tower.

Guests become assistant lighthouse keepers during their stay, learning about the history of the lighthouse and participating in helping to maintain the structure. Guests are asked to perform various keeper's duties, including sweeping the tower stairs, gardening, raising the flag, and making weather observations. The work helps maintain the historic structure and keep operating costs low. All proceeds from the B&B go to the restoration and maintenance of the lighthouse.

The B&B has three bedrooms and one common bathroom; each bedroom has a view of Lake Superior. The view from the Keeper's Room is framed by the front yard and outbuildings. The Harbor Room offers views of giant freighters as they come and go from the docks directly outside the window. The Forest Room faces east, with great views of the water and nearby woods. It is the largest of the rooms and can accommodate three people.

Guests have access to the living room and use of the kitchen on a limited basis. As a reflection of the heritage of the region, a Scandinavian-style breakfast is served each morning in the dining room. The signature item is a fruit soup. A keeper prepares the breakfast, but guests often pitch in to help.

Lighthouse Bed & Breakfast

1 Lighthouse Point
Two Harbors, Minnesota 55616
(218) 834–4814 or (888) 832–5606
www.lighthousebb.org,
www.lakecountyhistoricalsociety.org
E-mail: lakehist@lakenet.com

Rooms: Three bedrooms, shared bathroom.

Rates: Rooms are $125 per night and are for one or two people. There is a $25 charge for each extra person per night.

Season: Year-round.

Restrictions: No pets. No smoking. Please inquire regarding children younger than twelve.

Reservations: Reservations are held on a credit card; MasterCard, Visa, American Express, and Discover are accepted. Final payments are due upon check-in. Cash, checks, or credit cards are accepted for final payment. A gift certificate will be issued for cancellations with at least three days' notice. If the reservation is canceled within three days before your scheduled arrival date and the room is rebooked, you will received a gift certificate; otherwise you are responsible for the reservation.

Check-in/out: Check-in is between 3:00 and 5:00 P.M.; check-out is 11:00 A.M.

Other features: Small private luncheons, meetings, and family gathering are catered in the lighthouse dining room.

Other information: In addition to staying at the lighthouse, self-guided tours are available to visitors who are just passing through the area. Tours include a shipwreck exhibit, which features the pilot house of the *Frontenac,* an ore carrier that sank in Lake Superior in 1972. Tours are available May through October, Monday through Saturday from 9:00 A.M. to 5:00 P.M. and Sunday from 10:00 A.M. to 3:00 P.M. Winter tours may be arranged through the Lake County Historical Society office at (218) 834–4898. The cost is $2.50 for adults and $1.00 for children between the ages of nine and seventeen.

Directions: The Two Harbors Lighthouse Bed & Breakfast is about 30 miles north of Duluth. From US 61 in Two Harbors, turn on First Street toward the lake. Turn right on First Avenue and then left on Third Street. Continue to the end of the parking area. The lighthouse is located at the northeast end of the parking area.

THINGS TO DO

One of the best-known Great Lakes lighthouses is less than a half-hour drive north of Two Harbors. The **Split Rock Lighthouse and History Center** is situated on a dramatic cliff overlooking Lake Superior. Split Rock Lighthouse was built in 1910 to guide vessels along the north shore of the lake and into Two Harbors.

There is a wealth of outdoor recreational opportunities in the vicinity of the lighthouse. There are a number of hiking trails nearby, including the **Sonju Trail** around the lighthouse. Birding and nature walking are available on the nearby **Superior Hiking Trail.** In winter it is possible to cross-country ski, snowshoe, or snowmobile on a number of trails in the area.

Selkirk Lighthouse
Pulaski, New York

Built in 1838, the Selkirk Lighthouse served for only a short time. It was decommissioned in 1858 when the local fishing and shipbuilding industries declined. The lighthouse has been in private hands for nearly a century and a half.

Three keepers served at the Selkirk Lighthouse during its brief twenty-year history. Keepers were paid $350 for eight to nine months of service. During the winter they moved to their homes in Pulaski.

The lens rooms at the Selkirk Lighthouse is one of a few of its kind in the country. "We have one of only four remaining birdcage lanterns in North America," says owner Jim Walker. "This early style of lantern featured small panes of glass. Unfortunately, this design interfered with the beacon and made it difficult to see the light from any kind of distance offshore."

The lighthouse continues to operate as a private aid to navigation with a modern optic in the original birdcage lens room. Walker, who pays for the upkeep and restoration of the lighthouse with the income from rentals, is determined to preserve the structure's unique features.

STAYING THERE

Lighthouse fans, fishermen, and travelers looking for a noteworthy overnight experience can take advantage of the lodging at the Selkirk Lighthouse in Pulaski, New York. The lighthouse is located near the mouth of the Salmon River, where it flows into the far southeastern corner of Lake Ontario.

This is not a bed-and-breakfast inn. The completely furnished residence accommodates up to ten people. The lighthouse offers daily, weekly, and monthly rentals that are more of a housekeeping arrangement, with linens, blankets, kitchen utensils, and appliances provided. Guests provide their own food. The accommodations are clean but somewhat rustic, in keeping with the history of the lighthouse.

The lighthouse is a two-story waterfront home overlooking Lake Ontario and a working commercial harbor. Built of stone quarried nearby, it resembles an old stone farmhouse, except for the small lantern room jutting from the roof.

The first floor of the lighthouse has a completely renovated bath and shower, a small bedroom, and a combined kitchen/dining room with a modern double stainless sink, large refrigerator, gas stove, toaster, and coffeemaker. The second floor has two bedrooms and a large living room/bedroom that also can sleep two to three people.

The third floor is unfinished and unfurnished and is used for storage. Guests have access to the lantern room by way of a narrow wooden spiral staircase. A door leads to a railed walkway around the exterior of the lantern room and an excellent platform from which to view and photograph sunsets over Lake Ontario and the boating activity in the harbor.

Selkirk Lighthouse is known in some historic literature as the Salmon River Lighthouse. The river gets its name from the runs of Atlantic salmon that once were abundant in the area. The waters have been restocked with Pacific salmon, and many fisherman come to the area around the lighthouse to try to hook a big one when the salmon are running.

There is a gift and tackle shop at the lighthouse, and boat rentals and charters are available.

Selkirk Lighthouse

6 Lake Road Extension

P.O. Box 228

Pulaski, New York 13142

(315) 298–6688

Fax: (315) 298–6685

www.maine.com/lights

E-mail: jrwalker@ix.netcom.com

Rooms: Three bedrooms; maximum occupancy is ten people. Additional housekeeping accommodations are available on the premises.

Rates: Rates are for rental of the entire lighthouse by a group or family. You share the building only with those you bring with you. Sunday through Thursday, the cost is $125 for a party of two and $50 for each additional guest; Friday and Saturday, $150 for a party of two and $50 for each additional guest. Discounts are available for extended stays; call the reservation desk for a quote.

Season: Mid-April to mid-December.

Restrictions: No pets. No smoking.

Reservations: A 50 percent deposit is required within 10 days of the date the reservation is made. Visa, MasterCard, and American Express are accepted. Thirty days' cancellation notice is required for a refund. There is a $20 can-

The area near the Selkirk Lighthouse on Lake Ontario is known for its outstanding fishing.

cellation charge. A monthly schedule on the Web site shows availability. Typically, the lighthouse is at more than 90 percent occupancy over the eight-month season. Reservations are taken a year in advance.

Check-in/out: Check-in is 4:00 P.M.; check-out is 1:00 P.M.

Directions: Selkirk Lighthouse is 37 miles south of Watertown, New York, and 37 north of Syracuse. The location is accessible from both directions along I–81. Take exit 36 off I–81 and follow signs to Port Ontario.

THINGS TO DO

The primary recreational activity here is fishing. Because the lighthouse is located at the mouth of the Salmon River and on the shore of Lake Ontario, it is considered one of the best fishing locations in this part of the country. *Sports Afield* magazine has described the area within 300 yards of the Salmon River breakwater as one of the best places to fish in all of North America.

 ## Tibbetts Point Lighthouse
Cape Vincent, New York

The original 59-foot-high stone lighthouse tower was built at Tibbetts Point in 1827. It was replaced by a new 69-foot-high white-stucco conical tower built in 1854.

In 1896 a steam-powered fog signal was added to the light station. In 1917, the steam whistle was replaced by an air diaphone that ran on an automatic timer. A radio beacon later replaced the fog signal as an aid to shipping. The powerful signal, which could be heard for a distance of 4 to 5 miles, is still operable but no longer used.

The Fog Horn Building has a collection of historical items and offers an audio history of the lighthouse. A visitor center and lighthouse museum, operated by the Tibbetts Point Lighthouse Society, is open on weekends from Memorial Day through September, and daily during July and August.

The site was manned by the Coast Guard until 1981, when it was automated. The Coast Guard continues to service the light. Unfortunately, the lens is not accessible to visitors at this time, but you can get excellent photographs of the beautiful Fresnel lens in operation at night.

STAYING THERE

At the end of Tibbetts Point Road, where Lake Ontario meets the St. Lawrence River, the Tibbetts Point Lighthouse continues to assist ships traveling from the St. Lawrence Seaway into the Great Lakes. Ships from all over the world pass by the lighthouse along one of the busiest water routes in the Great Lakes. The tower at Tibbetts Point operates with its original fourth-order Fresnel lens, the only one of the classic lenses still in operation on Lake Ontario.

The Tibbetts Point Lighthouse Hostel offers an opportunity to spend a night in a historic Great Lakes lighthouse along the beautiful shoreline of Lake Ontario. The location is a great starting point for exploring New York's famous Thousand Islands region and nearby Canada.

The Tibbetts Point Lighthouse in Cape Vincent, New York, offers low-cost, family accommodations.

The low-cost accommodations are managed by Hostelling International. The mission of Hostelling International is "to help all, especially the young, gain a greater understanding of the world and its people through traveling." The hostel at Tibbetts Point Lighthouse attracts people interested in lighthouses and those seeking clean, affordable overnight quarters. Hostel manager Jean Cougler says families, young people, and many international guests enjoy a rewarding experience at the lighthouse.

The hostel has a total of twenty-six beds. Twenty of the beds are in the two-story former head lighthouse keeper's quarters built in 1880. Another six rooms are available in the assistant keeper's house, which was built in 1907 and also serves as the home for the resident manager. Guests share two bathrooms.

The dormitory-style rooms offer separate quarters for men and women. Private rooms are available for families. The hostel provides linens, blankets, and pillows. Guests must provide for their own food.

Given the attraction of the lighthouse, the limited space, the low cost, and the many tourist attractions in the region, the Tibbetts Point Lighthouse Hostel is often booked well in advance.

Tibbetts Point Lighthouse Hostel

33439 Country Route 6
Cape Vincent, New York 13618
(315) 654–3450
www.thousandislands.com,
www.hostellinginternational.org
E-mail: lighthousehostel@TDS.net

Rooms: Twenty-six rooms, two shared bathrooms.

Rates: $12 per night for members of Hostelling International, $15 per night for nonmembers. There is usually a three-night maximum stay, which can be extended with permission in advance from the manager.

Season: May 15 through October 25.

Restrictions: No pets. No alcohol. No smoking.

Reservations: Reservations are accepted only by phone. A check deposit is required within a week of making the reservation. No credit cards are accepted.

Check-in/out: Check-in is 5:00 to 9:00 P.M.; check-out is 7:00 to 9:00 A.M.; daily.

Other features: Shared kitchen facilities, lockers, parking, Internet access, common room with TV, outdoor picnic tables, chairs, and grills.

Other information: Office hours are 7:00–9:00 A.M. and 5:00–10:00 P.M.

Directions: From Syracuse take I–81 north to exit 46 at Watertown. Take State Route 12F and then 12E to Cape Vincent. Turn left on Broadway, and continue 2½ miles, until you reach the hostel. From Kingston, Ontario, take the ferry to Wolf Island and Cape Vincent, then drive 2 blocks to James Street. Turn right on Broadway.

THINGS TO DO

The Tibbetts Point Lighthouse serves as a gateway to the famous **Thousand Islands** of upstate New York and southeastern Ontario. The region stretches 50 miles from Cape Vincent to Ogdensburg. The St. Lawrence River widens as it meets Lake Ontario, becoming a world-renowned vacation paradise dotted with more than 1,800 islands ranging in size from mere points of rock to several square miles. The area is known for some of the best year-round sportfishing in the country.

Cape Vincent has the distinction of being the only community that still operates an automobile and passenger ferry across the St. Lawrence River to Canada. That puts **Kingston,** the oldest city in Ontario Province, within easy reach of visitors to the lighthouse. Kingston is a bustling city steeped in three centuries of grand Canadian history.

 # Apostle Islands Lighthouses
Wisconsin

There are six light stations in the Apostle Islands; four are staffed by volunteers. They offer an interesting mix of locations, amenities, architectural styles, and types of work experience.

Despite its remote location **Devils Island Light Station** is one of the more heavily visited lighthouses in the Apostle Islands. The 80-foot steel tower and residence is situated at the northernmost point in Wisconsin, overlooking an extensive formation of sea caves. Keepers can expect to climb the tower stairs many times on a summer weekend.

The brick Queen Anne–style keeper's house is about 300 feet from the tower. This is the only station with flush toilets and drinkable tap water. There are no electric lights, but the house has a propane heater, gas-powered refrigerator, and a gas stove for cooking.

There are several boat landings on Devils Island, so keepers are rarely stranded by weather, but it is sometimes necessary for keepers to carry supplies and gear as much as a mile from a landing site.

Outer Island Lighthouse is the most remote of the Apostle Islands light stations. Visitation is relatively sparse, and keepers must be prepared for isolation. The island offers unparalleled opportunities for hiking and exploration.

A passageway connects the two-story keeper's house to the 90-foot tower. The house is equipped with a 12-volt electric system to power the lights in the evening. There is running water for washing, but drinking water must be brought in from the mainland. The house has a propane heater, a gas-powered refrigerator, and a gas stove for cooking. Sanitary facilities consist of an outhouse.

Sand Island Lighthouse occupies a scenic, rocky promontory with spectacular views of the open lake. Visitation at the lighthouse is high, providing ample opportunities for volunteer keepers to share Sand Island's dramatic stories with visitors.

The lighthouse is a single structure, with living quarters attached to a low tower. Electricity is limited to one 12-volt light in the kitchen; there is no running water. Wash water is drawn from the lake, and drinking water is brought from the mainland. There is a propane heater, as well as a gas-powered refrigerator and a gas stove for cooking. Sanitary facilities consist of an outhouse. Volunteers must usually haul supplies 2 miles up a woodland trail from the nearest dock.

Michigan Island Light Station has two towers. One is the oldest of the Apostle Islands lighthouses; the other is the tallest. The island is remote, and visitation is relatively light. Because of the dock's exposed location, Michigan Island may at times be inaccessible by boat for a day or more, temporarily stranding volunteers on the island.

The keeper's quarters, a two-story brick house, has no electricity. There is a propane heater, a gas-powered refrigerator, and a gas stove for cooking. There is running water for washing, but drinking water is brought in from the mainland.

The National Park Service provides boat transportation to and from all of the island lighthouses, a two-way radio for communication, housing at the lighthouse, cleaning supplies,

The Outer Island Lighthouse is one of several light stations that offer accommodations in Wisconsin's Apostle Islands National Lakeshore.

training, and orientation. Full medical compensation is provided if you are injured on the job.

Volunteers are responsible for their own food, bedding, and personal items. Although there is no salary, the park does provide a limited reimbursement for mileage and expenses.

STAYING THERE

The scenic archipelago known as the Apostle Islands includes twenty-two islands and 12 miles of scenic shoreline jutting into Lake Superior at the northernmost tip of Wisconsin. It is an area of sandy beaches, sandstone cliffs, spectacular sea caves, remnants of old-growth forests, bald eagles, black bears, and one of the largest collection of lighthouses in a confined area in the United States.

The lighthouses that ring the edge of the Apostle Islands offer the most demanding lighthouse accommodations in America. The Apostle Islands National Lakeshore allows volunteers to serve as lightkeepers for several weeks or the entire summer at one of the four staffed lighthouses.

This is a tough summer stint on a remote island where a significant level of self-sufficiency is required, but the rewards are many if you have the time and inclination to take on the responsibility.

The duties for volunteer lighthouse keepers include greeting visitors and conducting interpretive guided tours of the light station, hiking island trails and performing light trail work, administering first aid to visitors, and providing an on-site presence to prevent vandalism of historic structures. Volunteers also mow lawns and perform routine grounds maintenance; perform light housekeeping, including sweeping and washing windows; and assist Historic Structures Preservation workers with planned maintenance projects.

The opportunity to stay and work at one of the Apostle Islands lighthouses attracts a diverse group of people. Many are older, retired individuals or couples, some are families with children, and others are young people. The park service is always looking for qualified people for the position of volunteer keeper, but they emphasize that it involves a lot of work and is not a summer vacation.

Apostle Islands National Lakeshore

Route 1, Box 4

Bayfield, Wisconsin 54814

(715) 779–3397

www.nps.gov/apis

Rooms: Four lighthouses with varying types of facilities.

Season: Mid-June through the end of September.

Restrictions: No pets allowed. Volunteers must be at least eighteen years old.

Reservations: To apply, e-mail the Volunteer Coordinator from the Web site, or call the park office. Applications are accepted throughout the year. Selections are usually made by March 31 for the following summer.

Other information: The Apostle Islands National Seashore Web site has a great deal of information about the volunteer program and about each of the lighthouses.

*Outer Island Lighthouse,
Apostle Islands National
Lakeshore, Wisconsin.*

ALPHABETICAL LISTING OF LIGHTHOUSES

LIGHTHOUSES BY TYPES OF ACCOMMODATIONS

Romantic B&Bs

Remote

Be a Lighthouse Keeper

Families/Groups

PHOTO CREDITS

Many thanks to the following people and organizations
for providing photos, with special thanks to Bruce Roberts,
coauthor of *American Lighthouses,* Second Edition
(The Globe Pequot Press, 2002): p. x, Isle au Haut, © Bruce
Roberts; p. 8, Hooper Strait, © Bruce Roberts; p. 18, Race
Point, courtesy of the Cape Cod Chapter of the American
Lighthouse Foundation; p. 22, Saugerties Lighthouse,
© Allen Emersonn, courtesy of the Saugerties Lighthouse;
p. 26, Rose Island, © Bruce Roberts; p. 32, Five Finger Island
Lighthouse, © Driftwood Productions; p. 33, Sentinel Island
Lighthouse, © Driftwood Productions; p. 35, Point Retreat,
© Driftwood Production; p. 36, East Brother, © Bruce
Roberts; p. 41, Pigeon Point, © Bruce Roberts; p. 44, Point
Arena Lighthouse, © Bruce Roberts; p. 51, Heceta Head Light
Station, © Bruce Roberts; p. 57, New Dungeness,
© Driftwood Productions; p. 60, North Head Lighthouse,
© Bruce Roberts; p. 69, Sand Hills Lighthouse, © Mary
Mathews, courtesy of Sand Hills Lighthouse; p. 71, Whitefish
Point, © Bruce Roberts; p. 79, Selkirk Lighthouse,
© Driftwood Productions; p. 80, Tibbetts Point, © Driftwood
Productions; p. 84, Outer Island Lighthouse, © Bruce
Roberts; p. 86, Outer Island Lighthouse, Apostle Islands,
© Driftwood Productions; p. 92, New Dungeness,
© Driftwood Productions.